MICHAEL
SHIELDS
MY STORY

M I C H A E L
SHIELDS
M Y   S T O R Y

Sport Media

WITH GREG O'KEEFFE

Sport Media

MICHAEL SHIELDS: MY STORY
By Michael Shields with Greg O'Keeffe

Production: Adam Oldfield, Michael Haydock

Produced by Trinity Mirror Sport Media:
Business Development Director: Mark Dickinson. Executive Editor: Ken Rogers.
Editor: Steve Hanrahan. Production Editor: Paul Dove. Art Editor: Rick Cooke.
Sales and Marketing Manager: Elizabeth Morgan.
Sales and marketing assistant: Karen Cadman.

Sub Editors: Roy Gilfoyle, Adam Oldfield, Michael Haydock.
Designers: Barry Parker, Colin Sumpter, Lee Ashun, Glen Hind, Alison Gilliland, Jamie Dunmore,
James Kenyon. Writers: Chris McLoughlin, David Randles, John Hynes, Gavin Kirk.

ISBN: 9781906802363

Photographs: Courtesy of the Shields family,
Trinity Mirror (Mirrorpix/Liverpool Daily Post & Echo), PA Pics.
Pictures of Michael in Liverpool and at the Shields' family home
by Colin Lane.
With thanks to Liverpool Football Club.

Printed in the UK by CPI Bookmarque, Croydon, CR0 4TD

Evil men testify against me and
accuse me of crimes I know nothing
about... may those who want to see
me acquitted shout for joy and say
again and again, 'How great
is the Lord.'

– Psalms 35

Bible passage highlighted by
Bishop of Liverpool James Jones on
visiting Michael Shields in a
Bulgarian prison

Contents

An Innocent Man

THE September sun beamed down on me as I walked through Liverpool city centre.

I tried to take in how different the city was from the one I left behind when I set off for Istanbul and glory in 2005.

It was Friday and the city had that end of the week buzz about it. People smiled as they saw me, many stopped to shake my hand. My family were waiting at home planning a big welcome home party.

I was with my friends easing back into the banter and jokes.

Now and then I had to stop and remind myself this was all real. The words of the prison Governor still rang in my ears.

"You're an innocent man. You're free."

I'd been through hell and back for four and a half years. Now I want to tell my story. Here it is.

Michael Shields,
Liverpool, 2009

I HAVE concluded, having looked carefully at all the evidence now available, that Michael Shields is telling the truth when he says he is innocent of the attempted murder of which he was convicted in Bulgaria. That being so I have recommended to Her Majesty the Queen that he should be granted a free pardon. Mr Shields is being released from prison today and will return home to his family a free man.

– Excerpt from statement made by
Justice Jack Straw, September 9, 2009

Preface

I answered a phone on the Liverpool Echo's news desk and it practically defined the next four years of my career. It was a night shift. The stressed voice on the other end of the line was Michael Shields senior and he was ringing to ask for our help. He wanted us to report what had happened to his son.

He'd been arrested in Bulgaria for attempted murder, he explained. The police had got the wrong man. Journalists get used to people bending the truth in order to get news coverage which suits them. But this man didn't sound like he was lying.

I filed a story for the next day's paper. It was to be the first of hundreds. From the first article, I began to run with the story. It had legs. It led me to Michael Shields' shoddy Bulgarian jail cell as the first journalist to interview him since his arrest. It led me to a face to face meeting with Jack Straw in a room at the North Liverpool community justice centre. It led me to breaking the exclusive when another man confessed. It led me back to Bulgaria a second time, and to a prison official foiling my plan to pose as Michael's cousin in order to get into his jail again. "Journalist," he said in broken English handing my passport back to me with a scowl. "No cousin. Journalist." He'd read the Echo online.

Finally it led me to a joyous car journey to Warrington's Thorn Cross prison on September 9, 2009 to pick up Michael Shields with his family and shake his hand as a free man.

This book would not have worked without Michael's courage, maturity, trust, friendship and patience. I hope I have told his story with the honesty and lack of self pity with which he shared it with me. It would not have worked without the generosity, support and strength of Maria and Michael snr. Not to mention the cups of tea and bacon sandwiches.

Thanks to my parents Liz and Steve, my brother Dom, my Nana and the rest of my family for their support. Also my friends and colleagues who put up with my rants about a miscarriage of justice and nicknamed me O'Shields.

I am obliged to Kevin Sampson who vouched for me as the author. To Emile Coleman, Tony Barrett and Paddy Shennan for the advice. The book flourished thanks to the calm reassurance, hard work and encouragement of Paul Dove, Steve Hanrahan and Ken Rogers at Sport Media. It was nurtured by the understanding of my editors Jane Haase, Maria Breslin and Alastair Machray.

Finally, I am grateful to Joe Anderson. A fellow Bluenose who kept me up to date with daily phone calls. He always said he would phone me first with the good news and when it came, as with everything, he was true to his word.

Greg O'Keeffe, Liverpool,
September 11, 2009

MICHAEL SHIELDS
MY STORY

1. A Nightmare
in Bulgaria

Excitement about going home wakes me up in the morning. On my first holiday abroad without my parents, I've seen Liverpool make history, and travelled through two countries, but now I'm ready to get back to my city and my family.

My suitcase is already packed and it's just a case of waiting. I've slept through breakfast but Kieran and John come up and say there are police downstairs taking everyone's passports from the hotel deposit safes.

I go downstairs just in case, and get our passports because our flight tickets are with them. We're sitting in the room when there's a knock on the door.

Three policemen walk in and tell us, in broken English, to put on white T-shirts, bring our passports, and follow them. We're worried and confused.

"What for?" we each ask.

But they are not interested in explaining anything and tell us to follow them now.

When we get to the lobby, the police stop and speak to each other before gesturing that they only want me, and usher me into a car. Suddenly scared, I ask Kieran and John to come with me. A lad who has come to see what's going on says something about making sure our stories match.

"What story? Match with what?" I'm thinking. "What the hell is going on?"

The police car is clammy and the leather seats are hot on my skin. We drive along the main strip, going past all the main bars, and stop outside a diner. Everything looks different in the harsh sun of mid-morning.

One of the policemen gets out and walks over to a group of people outside the diner. He points back at the car and they look over.

As he gets back in, I'm telling myself it'll be alright when I tell them about my night. I'm worrying about missing my flight when the car pulls up outside a police station. I'd expected to be taken back to the hotel.

They sit me in a chair and ask my name. 'You've got my passport there,' I think, getting grouchy as well as panicky.

I sit for hours, doing nothing, then a woman comes over. She is a translator and explains that I'm going in an ID parade.

'Great,' I think. 'After this I can go and get my flight home. The coach is due to pick us up at 6pm and if this goes quickly, I can still make it.'

I'm handcuffed to radiator pipes as I wait and the room had filled up, mostly with Bulgarian lads, but also the other Scouser I recognised.

He is handcuffed to the same radiator in the corner. We're too scared to speak much.

There are also three Bulgarians in white jumpers. I'm the only one in a T-shirt.

I'm a bag of nerves and confusion as we're made to line up in a small room opposite a two-way mirror. The first person walks in and stares right at me. He speaks in Bulgarian to the officer for a moment and then walks out.

A second person comes in and does the same thing.

A third enters and takes longer, looking at our faces. Scrutinising us.

The police spend longer talking to this man. Seeing my obvious horror and confusion, the translator asks me if I object to anything.

"Yes," I manage to say. "I wasn't even there. What's going on?"

It feels like I'm being stitched up.

I'm standing there next to three lads and I'm obviously the only English one.

My stomach is churning.

I'm in a T-shirt, they're in jumpers.

I'm led out of the room and back into the corner of the station, where I'm handcuffed to the radiator again.

Panic is coursing through my veins.

As people speak about me in Bulgarian, I'm desperate to know what they're saying.

I feel very alone and very frightened.

My mood lifts slightly when our tour rep comes in with a pair of tracksuit bottoms for me. She leaves quickly and comes back an hour later with some food.

I can only manage a few bites of the sandwich she's brought. I feel sick to the pit of my stomach.

My skin is bruised from where I've been laying on the cold, hard tiles, so she gave me some cushions to make us a bit more comfortable.

As soon as she leaves, the policeman comes and takes them away, smirking.

The rep said that most of our group had gone to get the flight home but the twins have stayed behind for me and they're in contact with my parents.

She said mum and dad were going to fly over. My flight has gone and I wasn't on it.

I FEAR FOR SON IN
BULGARIA PRISON
Exclusive By Mary Murtagh

A DREAM trip to watch Liverpool's Champions League triumph turned into a prison nightmare for Michael Shields.

The 18-year-old is being held in a Bulgarian jail for a crime he insists he did not commit.

He and two other teenage Reds fans from Liverpool are accused of hitting a young Bulgarian boy over the head with a brick and leaving him for dead.

But Mr Shields' friends say he was asleep in the same hotel room as them when the attack happened.

The Wavertree student has been held by police since Monday. His family fear he will be charged with attempted murder.

His father, also Michael, 45, said: "My worst fear is that he will be sent to a Bulgarian prison for something he hasn't done.

"Michael has never been in trouble in his life and I know he will be scared. We have not slept or eaten since Monday."

Mr Shields and six of his friends flew to Bulgaria on May 23, catching a coach to Istanbul for the match.

On the Sunday the friends had a few drinks in Bulgaria and went to bed at around 3.30am.

The friends have sworn statements to say he never left the room until 11.30am the next day – the attack happened outside a kebab shop at 5am.

The victim suffered life-threatening injuries but is now recovering in hospital.

Michael's family – dad Michael, 45, mother Maria, 45, sisters Melissa, 26, and Laura, 23 – are desperate for news.

A Foreign Office spokesman said: "If they are not charged they should be released.

"If not, our embassy staff will make representations to the Bulgarian authorities."

– Liverpool Echo, June 3, 2005

During the night as I lie there half-asleep trying not to doze off, a detective comes and takes my fingerprints.

He also produces a camera and takes my photograph.

The next day, he says, we are being moved to Varna to be charged. It's a nightmare I can't wake up from.

2. Scouser Born and Bred

I was only four years old when my dad first took me onto the Kop for a match against Norwich City. Maybe that day planted a seed in my young mind, because for a while afterwards I liked the Canaries almost as much as I was beginning to love Liverpool.

Now I'm Red through and through, but I liked Norwich that much for a while I even asked for one of their shirts one Christmas. They were playing well in Europe and I'd ask to watch them whenever the games were on TV. That's not all – another year I gave dad my list for Christmas presents and number one was an Arsenal top.

It's probably an understatement to say he was surprised, but I'd just taken a shine to Arsenal and liked the top. I even went on a school trip wearing my Gunners shirt.

Soon my dad's influence meant that Liverpool were my only team, and before long I could recite every song from the Kop. It was the start of an obsession and love for the club that will never leave me. It also meant that when we got to a European Cup final in 2005, I had to be there.

ANYONE WOULD BE PROUD TO HAVE HIM AS A SON
By Michael Shields Senior, Michael's dad

My two daughters are my world and I love them to bits, but when we found out Maria was pregnant a third time, I was desperate for a boy. Of course, the main thing is always that the babies are healthy, but all my brothers had boys and it had become a running joke in our family.

"You'll never make a lad, Michael," they'd tease me, and I was the butt of the jokes at every family gathering. They used to take their little luds to the match with them, and I thought it'd be nice to do the same one day.

When Michael was born it was like we'd won the lottery. That day my cousin was getting married and Maria wasn't due to give birth but had been a bit poorly and went into hospital at the last minute.

I went to the wedding but I was worried sick and kept popping out to phone the Oxford Street hospital. Every time I called there was no news except that Maria was OK, so I began to relax, then the last time I called I got a shock.

"You'd better get down here, Mr Shields," said the nurse. "She's having the baby."

By the time I got there, Maria was in the final part of her labour. I'd had a few drinks and was just in time for Michael to be born. Maria couldn't see the baby, and when I saw it, the first thing I looked for was a little willy! When I saw it was a boy, I was celebrating like a wild man.

I stayed in the hospital for a couple of hours, and then sprinted to Maria's parents' house at 4am to tell them the news. I was still buzzing, so then I went and woke up my mum and dad to tell them, too. I had a boy.

The year he was born, Liverpool did the double. We won the league at Chelsea and beat Everton in the FA Cup final. What a year I'd had. I'd got the son I had been waiting for and Liverpool were winning trophies.

He was born two weeks premature and only weighed 5lbs 7oz. Pretty soon he had a head of blond hair and was a cute kid, but he would never smile for photographs. Maria and I would be standing on our heads trying to get a smile out of him, but he wasn't interested.

He was a good kid and never caused any trouble, but he suffered with his ears and had to wear grommets. I remember going to nursery once to pick him up and the nurse said she was concerned about how quiet Michael was. She said he just sat there as if he wasn't listening. She asked me if we'd had his hearing checked so we took him to the hospital.

They told us what the problem was and it suddenly clicked. He'd had to lip-read without knowing he was doing it and thankfully the nursery had spotted it.

I remember on one holiday when he was young in Majorca I had hold of his hand as we walked along the strip one night. We spotted a hotel restaurant that seemed lively and I let go of his hand because he wanted to play with his toy camera.

The two girls followed me when I went to look inside the restaurant and Michael wandered off. We panicked big time. We were crying with fear and blind panic. We found him only about 15 yards away from us a few minutes later, surrounded by people, crying his little heart out. He wasn't allowed out of our sight after that.

Ironically, we also took the kids on holiday to Sunny Beach in Bulgaria when they were young. We had a lovely time and even went for a day trip to Golden Sands where he was arrested.

The Bulgarians were lovely people and we said we'd definitely go back. That's why we thought he'd be OK when he asked us if he could go to Bulgaria before the European Cup. We weren't keen to let him go, but we knew it was a nice place.

Every Sunday morning I used to take Michael with me to my mum and dad's house on Lodge Lane. As we walked, he'd ask me to sing Liverpool songs to him. It was at the time when the 'Anfield Rap' record was out and he'd pester me to sing that to him, especially the bit about Ian Rush.

"Sing it again, dad," he'd say. "Sing it again."

By the time I would get to my mam's, I'd be exhausted with him and he'd start on his granddad, telling him all the songs he'd learned.

"Well your dad won't remember this one..." he'd reply, and sing all the really old Liverpool songs. Michael was fascinated and I treasure those memories.

When he was a child, Liverpool weren't really winning much, but he was enamoured with the size and noise of Anfield. He just loved the Reds and used to worship John Barnes.

On another holiday we enjoyed in Majorca, he would refuse to take his Liverpool top off despite the heat.

He would be running around the pool singing Ian Rush songs all day, and we met a gang of young lads from Portsmouth who thought he was great.

They used to sit him on the bar and sing Portsmouth songs to him, and 'Lucky, Lucky, Lucky Liverpool...', and Michael would reply back about John Barnes.

He went to St Anne's primary school in Overbury Street and the first thing he'd do when he got home was change into his Liverpool top. Michael wasn't allowed to play outside on his own because we lived on a main road, so I'd take him to Botanic Park and play football with him. At the same time, Mike Tyson was in his prime and my dad would watch the fights with Michael on telly. He'd ring me and ask if "the little fella" was ready to come around, and he'd set up a little bed for him and stock up on lemonade and crisps.

I think Michael and I have hardly ever had a crossed word. Anyone would be proud to have him as a son. I've only had to raise my voice to him once when he was about 14 and wanted to go to an away match. He was upset because I'd said he was too young. He wanted to go to Manchester City but there had been hooligan trouble at their ground and I didn't want to risk it.

Michael was only three when I went to Hillsborough and escaped from the crush on the Leppings Lane, but as he got older, he was curious. "What happened, dad?" he'd ask. "How did you get away?" He quizzed me about Heysel, too. He had a very inquiring mind and loved all sports. He'd even sit up and watch the rugby and cricket.

I couldn't believe it when he was 11 and he asked me for an Arsenal top. He said he just liked the design of it.

I took him to his first FA Cup final when he was 10 against Manchester United in 1996. It was the year of the Spice Boy suits when we lost 1 0. Just before Cantona scored he said to me: "It's a terrible game this dad. Cantona has done nothing." He was crying when he came out of the ground because he saw all the Manchester United fans celebrating, but I told him we'd have our day.

I'm a window cleaner and I used to work Saturday mornings and then come home at about midday and get Michael ready to go to Anfield. I'd have a quick wash and something to eat and then have to drag him out of bed.

Other times I'd take him to work with me for pocket money to go to the match. He'd wipe all the window ledges down and I'd give him a few quid a week and my customers would, too. It was to teach him the value of work and earning money. He'd come home with bags of sweets and a few quid in his pocket, smiling from ear to ear.

His first season ticket was when he was about 15 in the Paddock and I used to meet him outside the cake shop after every game. I'd be standing there waiting for him for ages to dawdle along without a care in the world as everyone else walked past. He is so laid back. He was 17 when we first let him go to away games and we'd pick him up straight from the Barnes Travel coach. I remember he went to Newcastle and was amazed at how big St James's Park was.

My first game without him after he'd been arrested in the May was hard. After the game I stopped for a moment by the cake shop to wait for him. It was just an automatic thing... then I realised.

I saw lots of lads the same age and build with similar hair to him walking past. It was horrible. People would be coming up to me shaking my hand at the match and asking about Michael. They'd play 'You'll Never Walk Alone' and I'd be numb.

My mind would be racing, thinking: 'If I hadn't got Michael into football he wouldn't be where he is now.' I blamed myself. Then I was thinking: 'If my dad hadn't taken me to watch football, I wouldn't have got Michael into it. What if I'd supported Everton?' All those thoughts ran through my mind constantly. Michael said to me himself one day, though: "Dad, it could have been anyone."

IT'S PUSHED US TO THE BRINK
By Maria Shields, Michael's mum

Michael went to Campion High School. He was a shy teenager and conscious of his uneven top teeth, so we took him to have a brace fastened which would correct them. He was due to have the brace taken off for good at the Dental Hospital two days after he was supposed to be home from Bulgaria.

He made some good friends in Campion and Michael's cousins, the Graney twins, went there too. He used to get some lovely reports from the teachers and liked history and geography lessons.

While he was at school he used to say he'd like to write about sport for the Echo. He'd always grab the paper when we bought it to read the football news.

He'd spend a lot of time in his room when he was a teenager. Sometimes his mates would knock for him to see if he wanted to go and play out, but often he'd say he couldn't be bothered.

He was comfortable in his own company. In many ways, I think that's how he has coped. Michael (Senior) and I have both suffered every day since he was arrested. It's pushed us right to the brink and at times we've struggled to cope.

Michael was bright, but instead of staying on, he wanted to leave school at 16 and get a trade. He signed up for college to get on a course and when he couldn't get onto a plumbing or electrician traineeship, he signed up as a mechanic.

He did well on the course and was highly thought of by the staff, but it just wasn't for him. He left and started working as an engineering trainee on the railways, usually at Lime Street or in Garston. I remember when he walked into the living room for the first time in big rubber boots and overalls. He looked so grown up.

I kept praying to hear the sound of his keys in the front door. I prayed for the day he walked into the house as a free man and didn't have to go back to prison.

You torture yourself with silly ifs and buts about what happened in 2005.

What if Liverpool hadn't won it on penalties? What if that equalising goal hadn't gone in?

Even: What if he hadn't gone to Bulgaria?

Michael had passed his driving test shortly before he went to Bulgaria. He used the money he'd been saving from his wages to pay for his ticket and flights, but he'd actually been saving up for a car.

"I can save up again for a car when I get back, mum," he said. "I can't miss Liverpool in a European Cup final. I might not get the chance again."

Michael was brought up to know the difference between right and wrong. He's a good lad. Even as a young boy we didn't let him hang about on street corners. If he was going to his friend's house for tea, we wanted to know who the parents were and speak to them. We wanted to know who our children were with.

He was brought up to be polite and helpful. That's probably why he agreed to help the police in Bulgaria with those early ID parades. He thought he was just helping and would be able to go home later that day.

3. The Road to Istanbul

I was outside our house at 9.20am as arranged, buzzing with excitement.

I had my flag ready, my suitcase packed, my passport in my pocket and my money was safe. The all-important match ticket was safely tucked in my zipped-up coat pocket and the plan was to pick up the flight tickets at the airport.

Walking the short distance to my mate Spud's house, all I could think about was seeing Liverpool in the European Cup final and all the fun we'd have.

Spud was ready too, and he'd got the train tickets. Alan, another one of the lads, was going to be picking us up in a while.

I headed back to my house and my big sister Melissa asked me if I was excited.

"Of course I am," I said grinning. "You should know – it's all I've gone on about for weeks."

Then my mum came in and said she'd been allowed to leave work early to come and wave us off. I was glad.

A horn beeped outside and it was time to go. Mum had tears in her eyes and was putting a bag filled with sweets into my suitcase, just in case I didn't like the food over there.

The horn beeped again impatiently so I said my goodbyes and carried my suitcase out to the van. I waved to my mum, who was still a bit upset, and our Mel before jumping in.

"This is it," I thought. "My first Champions League final. Istanbul here we come."

Our plan was the same as loads of other Reds. To get to Bulgaria first and then to go to Istanbul from there. We knew Bulgaria would be full of Scousers, the only problem from there was how to actually get to the match.

Alan's brother Liam dropped us off at Lime Street station in the city centre. We jumped out and Spud was running through things.

"Train tickets?"

"Yes," we both replied.

"Match tickets?"

"Yeah."

Finally, looking at Alan, he said: "Match tickets?"

Alan's face dropped. He realised he'd left them in the glove box of the van.

"Shit, shit, shit," he said, panicking. "How am I gonna get in touch with our Liam?"

He tried to phone Liam but his phone was off. Finally, he managed to get hold of his aunty who, in turn, got hold of Liam, who, thank God, came back.

We jogged into Lime Street just in time to see the first train we could have taken pulling away from the platform. It wasn't the end of the world. Another train was due to leave in an hour that could take us to Preston, where we'd switch for the Glasgow train.

It was a great bunch of lads I was going with. Me, Spud, Powelly, Kieran, then two lads I didn't know as well: Alan and John. Instantly I got on with them – they were sound lads.

The plan was for John to share a room with Kieran and me.

We finally got on our train to Preston and the banter started while we read our magazines. The short journey went fast and we all jumped off at Preston to check when we could get the Glasgow train.

It was 11.20am, which was fine and meant we'd only have to wait for half an hour.

"Get the flag out Smick," Powelly shouted at me. So we unravelled it there in the middle of the station. It read:

'CHAMPIONS LEAGUE 05
KENNY LADS'

We were buzzing but also proud of our effort and imagining it draped over one of the stands at the Ataturk Stadium.

Next thing, the Glasgow train arrived, so we jumped on it, putting our cases on the overhead racks. Only another little train ride and we'd be in Scotland.

We got to Glasgow and found two taxis to Glasgow airport. Me, John and Kieran in one – Spud, Alan and Powelly in the other.

We started speaking to the cabbie – a Celtic fan who was devastated because they had just been pipped to the Scottish league by Rangers.

We were all Celtic fans in the back, asking him where they went wrong, and we got on to the topic of whether Liverpool had enough to beat AC Milan in the final. We were all sure we could.

At Glasgow airport we collected our flight tickets and checked in our suitcases. It was a great feeling when that was all done. We could relax and look forward to the plane.

To kill some time we went for something to eat in the restaurant, had a few games in the arcade and even a ride in the massage chair, which had us all in stitches.

There was only really time after that to do a little shopping in the Celtic shop and then we were on the plane.

I don't mind flying, but flights do seem to drag on and on. We were only on the plane for four hours but it felt like 10. John and I decided to have a beer on the plane, our first drink of the trip and then, after a rough landing, we were in Bourgas.

It was quite late. My suitcase was the first off, and before long everyone had theirs.

As we were getting on the coach to take us to our resort, Kieran spotted a flash of lightning. Nobody believed him at first but then, sure enough, more flashes appeared and we had to drive through the storm.

After an hour of driving in darkness lit up by these fizzing cracks of thunder and lightning, we stopped off at this moody little shop with loads of people sitting around at 3am like it was the middle of the day.

Some of us went for a quick burst in the toilets before getting a drink. Moody or not, we couldn't get over how cheap it was as we stocked up.

Back on the coach, the lightning was getting worse. At times the night sky was weirdly bright as flash after flash went by. Then the rain started; light at first, but soon it was coming down in sheets, battering against the roof of the coach.

Just for good measure, it started hailing, too. The hammer blows became more like a battering ram.

It wasn't frightening, but it was unsettling. We passed a car on a nasty looking bend which had crashed.

There were police all over the scene. We were all shitting ourselves and there was no banter.

Apart from the smashing hailstones, it was eerily quiet.

Finally, we reached a city and thought we were there. A little cheer even went up as we spotted a bar with the Playboy sign outside, but the coach just went on and it was another 20 minutes of boredom until we eventually reached Golden Sands.

After two hours of sitting on the coach, we were there. As Kieran checked us in, John went and bought a few drinks. The others walked tiredly to their rooms.

'We started off this morning and we've only just got here in the early hours of the next,' I thought, 'but what the hell – we're in Bulgaria.'

Our room was number 419 and Spud and the others were in 411. Standing on the balcony, I suddenly heard a familiar voice. It was my cousin Paul. I didn't even have a clue he was in the same part of Bulgaria as us, never mind the same hotel.

I was made up as I realised he was even on the same floor as us. They'd been at a karaoke bar and were only getting in at 5am. One of them, Garro, told me all about their night.

We all tried to get our heads down but we were too excited about going to Istanbul to sleep much. The only problem was how we were going to get there.

My phone alarm went off. It was 9am and soon we were all downstairs planning how to get to Turkey. We were not even bothered if we got there 24 hours early – we just wanted to be there.

The young rep at our hotel didn't have a clue, but a senior rep explained that she could get us to Bourgas and then on a coach to Istanbul for £70. It would get there on the Tuesday night or in the early hours of Wednesday.

A lad from another group didn't think much of her idea.

"She's rigging that," he said. "Rip-off."

So we carried on thinking how to get there on Tuesday.

About 12pm we got speaking to these fellas in our hotel who said that there should be coaches leaving from Bourgas every 30 minutes and they were cheaper than what the rep was saying.

We only had to get from our resort to Varna, 10 minutes away, to get on one. It was some kind of public holiday when we arrived in Varna, with parades and marches snaking through the centre.

The tourist information centre was shut. Our group was bigger now, as two lads from the hotel, Geoff and Ian, were coming with us.

Time for a different plan. We got a cab to Varna airport.

"I bet you any money the airport is like Speke used to be," one of them said. They were right, only at least Speke had aeroplanes.

We rushed into the building and looked up at the screens, scanning them for Istanbul, but no joy.

None of the staff spoke English and we ran about like headless chickens, before one of our brainier members realised we were looking at arrivals and not departures.

Feeling a bit thick, we resumed our search until we struck lucky and found a young woman with black hair who could speak English (she even understood Scouse!) and she said there were no planes to Istanbul.

Waste of time.

Back into yet another cab and back to Varna centre. We were not giving in – we WOULD get to Istanbul. We'd resorted to asking random people how to get to coaches, but nobody understood. A beggar shuffled over and we even tried to coax a bit of information out of him.

He pointed down the road and tried to make us follow him, but Alan thought he was just after money, so we walked away.

A few yards down the road we heard a foreign voice boom out: "LIVERPOOL." It was a taxi driver who'd done a u-turn and stopped dead in the middle of the road. As we walked over, we saw a nice fella called Bernie from our hotel. He was in the back with his wife.

Bernie knew we were having a nightmare and told us to go down the road and he would meet us there. A coach firm was running trips to Istanbul from there. Finally! It seemed like we were not the only Scousers panicking over getting to Istanbul.

At least it was organised panic, and there was someone selling coach tickets. We were all bouncing around when we were finally sorted at 5pm.

We had something to eat and then went back to the hotel to get ready for one last journey before the biggest game of our lives.

We were standing waiting for the coach, willing the minutes away. So excited. We'd all had our picture taken with my flag when Bernie got his out. What a cracker – it read:

> *'CARRA COMES FROM BOOTLE*
> *GERRARD FROM THE BLUEBELL*
> *NOW WE'RE DOWN TO ISTANBUL*
> *TO LIFT THE CUP IN HELL'*

We all had to have our picture taken with that and we noticed a fella who looked like Antonio Nunez, Liverpool's winger, so we got him on the pictures as well.

When the coach pulled up, we all bundled straight on and headed right for the back like big kids.

I had my own two seats to myself and Kieran passed me a can of lager once he'd settled down. We were looking at getting to Istanbul at about 3am.

The steward on the coach had already warned us that we were likely to get stuck on the border for two hours while there were checks.

We weren't bothered. The mood was relaxed and we were having a laugh. We went past a prison as we drove through Bulgaria and it looked horrible. There were watchtowers and grim barbed wire everywhere. We all agreed it was somewhere none of us would ever like to spend a minute.

We got to the border about midnight. At Bourgas we'd picked up a fella called Tony who was pretty drunk but a great laugh.

He was staying at a hostel like us but, unlike us, the poor lad didn't have a ticket for the match yet. I had mine ready to show customs when we came to the border.

A Bulgarian customs official came onto the coach and checked all our passports and asked to see everyone's match tickets. We helped the lads without tickets by passing our tickets back to them.

We couldn't see anyone get left behind or miss out.

Then it was on to another desk where we payed £10 for a temporary Visa and then into duty free to buy some more beers for the final leg of the trip.

The next four hours dragged, but Istanbul was at the front of all our minds and each motorway sign said it was fewer and fewer kilometres away. As we pulled into the coach station, it dawned on us that we didn't really know what to do or where to go next.

One bloke was telling everyone to get to Taksim Square and we recognised that place, so we took what felt like our 100th taxi of the trip so far.

4. Best Day Of My Life

Taksim Square was not as busy as we expected. There were two men waving Liverpool flags which we hadn't spotted before, but as we walked down towards all the hotels, it wasn't exactly bouncing. Yet...

Instead there were little groups of fans singing and a lot – and I mean a lot – of kebab shops, so we got one each and tucked in. Finding a hotel room for eight of us with kebab all over our tired faces wasn't easy.

Two Scousers, who were about the same age as us, said they were staying in rooms above an Irish bar, so we went looking for that. We tried street after street but couldn't find that bar. We were knackered and more than a bit fed up, so we just decided to stay in the square all night.

It was about 4.30am and we went and sat by some Liverpool fans who were singing. As much as we wanted to join in, we were shattered. You'd probably have thought we were a right bunch of boring sods because we were just sat there on top of our cases taking it all in as the singing went on and on.

As the majority of fans in the square started to drift back to their hotels, there were only about six left next to our group. Lots of Turkish lads started to come over and we suddenly didn't feel so safe. The tired excitement quickly wore off as we realised they were up to no good despite pretending to mingle.

One of the Turkish lads was trying to pick-pocket a middle-aged woman with the remaining fans, and the atmosphere went from dodgy to downright bad.

Another one of the Turks started arguing with the pick-pocket, who ended the row with a right hook. Thankfully, the woman knew about a place, the Hotel Info nearby, and we abandoned our plan to sleep in the square and followed the woman and her husband.

Somehow we got two rooms for 50 lira and they were great. We each sunk into bed for at least a little sleep before the day of the game.

The next morning we all looked really rough. We got up about 10.30am and had a quick wash before getting ready. The sun was streaming in through the hotel window, though, making us feel better by the moment.

Along with Geoff and Ian, I headed to reception and asked them to phone Kieran and John's room. It took 10 minutes for them to get downstairs and then we went outside and headed back to the square. I didn't know it then, but that sunny morning was the start of the best day of my life.

The square was transformed that day. Thousands upon thousands of Scousers, flags draped everywhere you looked. Then I spotted my cousin Joe's flag with, sure enough, him standing next to it.

We were all together then and the weather was roasting hot. Cans of the Turkish beer, Efes Pilsen, were being passed about and a festival was starting outside the stadium at 4pm.

Kick-off wasn't until 10.45pm, so we agreed to head to the ground for 6pm or 7pm – leaving six hours of fun ahead in Taksim.

A van pulled up in the centre and immediately a few lads jogged over. We followed in an instant as it dawned on us that it was the beer van – and it was filled with crates of cold Efes waiting to be dished out.

Beers in hands, we headed into the McDonald's a couple of yards away, and then spotted some of the lads clambering up onto the roof. Naturally we followed them until we were all singing and dancing above the roof next to the Golden Arches and scanning the mass of red. I'd never experienced an atmosphere like it.

Buses started arriving to take us to the ground, so we piled on. Locals were lined up on the streets watching us, probably shocked at the degree to which the buses were practically bouncing along.

The ground didn't look much as we pulled up next to a long line of identical coaches all stuck in a jam. It was just two stands in the middle of nowhere. Our bus was going nowhere, so we got off and started walking the short distance to the ground, over big mud hills and scrappy waste ground. I was wearing flip-flops so my feet were covered in black dust, but I wasn't bothered. We clambered over one last mud slope and saw scenes more like a rock concert than a footy match.

There was a big stage and different bands performing with loads of people singing along and dancing. We could tell it'd be easy to get onto the biggest stage, so we did. We stormed it. One lad had a Carragher flag and his mate was bowing down and kissing it. Flares were blasting off everywhere and I had to shake myself again – what an experience.

A Turkish announcer's voice boomed out over the PA telling everyone to get off the stage, but we couldn't move, we were laughing so hard.

Time was flying and we had to get into the ground. As we walked through the turnstiles, I saw my cousins, the twins, and caught up with them as we waited to be waved in.

Even in the queue the Ataturk still only looked like two stands, but once inside, I realised it was below ground level and it was gigantic.

Weeks of planning, days of travelling, very little sleep and here I was – at a European Cup final. All worth it to say I'd been at one. I went and fastened my flag to the netting in front of the first few rows of our section. We were standing about 20 rows up and slightly to the left of the goal.

It was 20 minutes until kick-off and the whole ground seemed to be red apart from a section by the bottom which didn't even seem to be sold out. We watched the opening ceremony impatiently as little kids in the respective kits got into the two team formations, but eventually the teams came out and the stadium shook. I still don't think there's a feeling like watching your team walk out in the European Cup final.

Things started going wrong shortly after the kick-off when Traore gave away that free-kick. You just knew something was going to happen and, sure enough, we were 0-1 down. We remained optimistic despite Liverpool doing nothing, and the only plus point was Harry Kewell limping pathetically off.

We all remember how well his replacement did. 0-2 came inevitably and we could feel the game slipping away, so I went to get some drinks. I heard another roar and instinctively knew it wasn't a Liverpool goal. In my head it was all over.

Half-time and we were feeling deflated. Actually, we were absolutely sick. Another half of humiliation looked a distinct possibility.

We could only play for pride at that point. 'You'll Never Walk Alone' rang out and a spirited chant of 'We're Gonna Win 4-3' emerged.

"If we score in the first 10, anything can happen lad," I said to Spud with forced enthusiasm.

He didn't answer. Deep down it was a pipe dream.

More than anything it was a relief to see Hamann come out for the second half, but our minds were straying to the long journey home facing us in three-quarters of an hour.

Nothing could ever prepare you for what happened next.

1-3 and I was still refusing to believe it could happen, 2-3 and I'm daring to dream. 3-3 and … well, it was chaos.

When Dudek made that save from Shevchenko you just knew it was fate for us to win.

One of the twins – Joey – came over to stand with us during the penalties, and he had everyone flapping. He couldn't stay quiet.

It took a minute for it to sink in after Dudek pulled off that all-important save. Even as we danced and watched with pride as Carragher and Gerrard lifted that cup, we still couldn't quite believe it.

It felt like I was flying as we left the ground. Lads were running up to the TV cameras shaking their fists in joy, and as I got bustled along with the euphoria, my leg somehow got trapped in a little barrier causing me to flip over onto the ground.

There was a big slap as I hit the deck and an instant of pain, but I sprang right back up. I felt invincible.

We zoomed over the mud slopes again, our legs full of energy despite the conditions. Then it was time to try and force ourselves onto any coach we could.

Seeing Spud make a dart, I followed him and launched myself at the nearest one which looked ready to pull away. I pressed the button just in time; the doors opened and we were both on.

Back at Taksim Square, we looked for the rest of them. I saw two mates from school and to escape the chaos for a bit, three of us went and sat in the lounge of a nearby hotel, but soon it was too quiet, so we headed back to the square.

After a bit of messing about, we found some of the lads and

headed to a pub that was absolutely bouncing, and outside were Kieran and John still talking about the match. Sunrise came and went with us still there, soaking up the atmosphere and mingling with Fenerbahce fans who were partying like they'd won it.

It started to get light, so we headed for our hotel. As we walked through the doors, everyone was lying in heaps fast asleep where they'd sunk to the floor. Much-needed sleep followed.

I woke up feeling strangely refreshed and walked outside alone. There were still fans everywhere, all smashed and gobbling kebabs at 6am. Back inside, Spud and Powelly had woken up, too, and straight away conversation returned to the game.

It was nearly 7am and thoughts turned to the journey back to Bulgaria. Our taxis to the coach station sped past big yellow and blue Fenerbahce flags, on proud display after they had won the Turkish league the week earlier.

As we settled into our seats on the coach, I felt as if we hadn't really celebrated properly. Maybe the celebrations just hadn't begun yet.

Ten long, long hours later, we were back in Varna and back at our hotel, the Kristal. I went into the bathroom to throw cold water onto my face and caught my reflection in the mirror. I hadn't slept properly for days and my feet were caked in mud.

But the news was that the homecoming parade was being shown on a big screen in an Irish bar later. I took a long, hot shower, put on some clean clothes and phoned home – then I was ready to go out.

It was bittersweet watching the homecoming from the bar. It was busy and the atmosphere was good, but we wanted to be there. We wanted to be lining the streets of Liverpool with our families, soaking it up outside St George's Hall.

Instead of feeling sorry for ourselves, we sang and went and had a laugh on a bouncy castle outside the pub. Several Efes later, we were in Muppets karaoke bar singing 'Ring of Fire' until late before our beds called again.

Daytime while we were in Varna was made for sleeping before going out again. Deep down I was feeling a bit homesick and counting the days until I could get home and see my dad. I phoned home whenever I could.

The routine was to sleep in until about 1pm, get out so the maid could clean the room, and have a dip in the pool. Then it'd be back for another forty winks before getting dressed to go out all over again. It was my first holiday abroad without my family.

Preparing for Friday night, the twins bounced into our room and said the plan was to head back to Muppets. More of the same. We'd all have happily pressed rewind and play on that night. As we sauntered through the lobby, we saw Bernie and his wife. He couldn't stop grinning and said he'd see us there.

BOOOOOOM!

Our small talk was interrupted by a loud bang and we all flinched. Turning around, we saw another Scouser with a huge drum which he was whacking with a vengeance. The hotel staff were begging him to stop it and then one of the security guards confiscated it.

As we were leaving, someone slipped into the room where the drum had been left and liberated it again. We walked down the main strip to the sound of victory drums, each step making us swell with pride.

We got to the little bar opposite Muppets and brought the place alive. The other, non-Scouse holidaymakers must've been made up because we turned every night into a party.

On our way back to the hotel after another classic Muppets night, we stopped at a bar which was showing the final again. Liverpool were 0-2 down as we got there, and it was as if we were watching it live again.

The place erupted when we won on penalties again. Back in bed, it was impossible to sleep. You'd drift off but then the singing would start again. No wonder we slept like logs in the daytime.

Saturday we had an easy night. The week was starting to catch up with all of us. Some of us played darts and others went on the internet and read about the homecoming.

Meanwhile, Spud was up to something. Someone told him to head over to room 309 because there were some birds waiting for him. We sneaked after him, trying to stifle our laughs but he saw us and he came and sat with us instead. It was probably a wind up anyway.

The next morning, after breakfast, we flipped through the hotel guest book. Someone had written:

> *'This is a nice hotel but it was ruined by the noise of the Liverpool fans who haven't shut up once.'*

We crossed out the name of the moaner and wrote *'from A. Ferguson'* in its place.

I was a bit surprised people were complaining. We never went overboard in the hotel at night and we'd just won the cup after all. That day we went to the beach for the first time we'd been at Golden Sands and we enjoyed it, staying for hours. Back in our room, we were getting ready to go out, but the consensus was to take it easy because we were going home the next day.

I rifled through the last of my clean clothes and put on a beige top and black shorts; I was saving my red top for going home.

Muppets was bouncing as ever, Bon Jovi's 'Livin' On A Prayer' seeming to be on repeat. We rolled on to a nightclub called Bonkers, but me and Geoff came out after half an hour. Tired again, we walked up to the hotel and had a drink in the bar. As I headed up to my room, I heard a girl's voice and walked in to find Kieran in there with a bird.

"We'll be downstairs mate," I said, smiling.

A little bit later, as me and Geoff were down in the bar, Kieran came down and I told him I'd be going to bed soon. He handed me the key card but wanted to go back out, so we jammed open the door of our room and I gave him the card back.

"That bird's still asleep in our room lad, just in case you get a shock," he said.

"I'm not arsed," I said, feeling sleepy. I went into the room and collapsed into one of the beds. Sleep came fast and heavy.

5. Varna – The Nightmare Continues

After the darkest night of my 18 years, spent in a cell still wondering what the hell was going on, I was shaken awake and told I had to sign papers. I was immediately reluctant. What were they? Was it some sort of confession? 'No way I'm signing,' I thought.

When the tour rep came, she phoned the embassy on her mobile and said it was OK for us to sign the papers, but I was panicking again.

"Get the tapes from the CCTV cameras in the hotel," I told her. "They'll show me in the hotel and the computer in the reception will have recorded my key card being used at about 2.30am. That's all you need to prove I wasn't at this fight."

I said it time and time again. Pleading with her.

"I'll get them checked," is all she said.

We got to Varna and waited again until two detectives came in and explained we were being formally charged. It was me and two other Scousers: Anthony Wilson and Bradley Thomson had also been arrested. The other Scouse lad they'd picked up (who I later realised to be Graham Sankey) had been released. A lawyer in a crumpled suit told each of us to say nothing.

My head felt like it was going to burst. I wanted to scream and make them understand that I didn't know what had happened.

I kept looking at the lawyer while the cold, hard voice of one of the detectives explained the rules and regulations of the detention centre we were being taken to. He looked worried. I never saw him again.

Next, the three of us were split up and I was taken upstairs and searched. The sound of a cell door opening acted as a jolt.

'Get your head together,' I tried to tell myself. I'd been in a daze but needed to be sharp.

SHOCK NEWS FOR CITY FAMILY
By Greg O'Keeffe

A TEENAGE Reds fan locked up in a Bulgarian jail was today charged with attempted murder.

Michael Shields, 18, of Wavertree, is accused of attacking a 25-year-old Bulgarian in a brawl at the Golden Sands resort.

Police also charged a second Liverpool teenager, 19-year-old Anthony Wilson, with hooliganism and possessing drugs, after the alleged attack last month.

The astonishing development comes as the Echo publishes heart-breaking letters to his mother revealing his inner turmoil.

– Liverpool Echo, June 27, 2005

We soon arrived at Varna detention centre for what was to be the longest month of my life.

It was in the middle of the city centre on the second floor from the top. I was led to a cell and pushed inside. Three beds and three people on top of them already. The only window was thick, like porthole glass on a ship. A green mouldy sheen over the glass meant nobody could see outside anyway.

At first, the three fellas in the cell looked at me, but then they carried on talking in a foreign language.

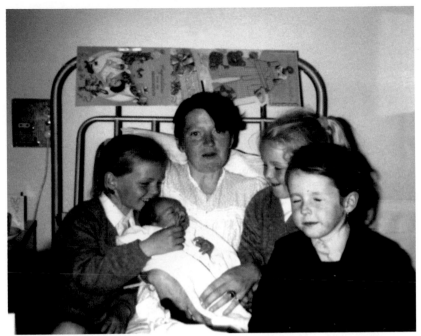

Michael Jnr: My arrival into the world – Monday, September 21st, 1986

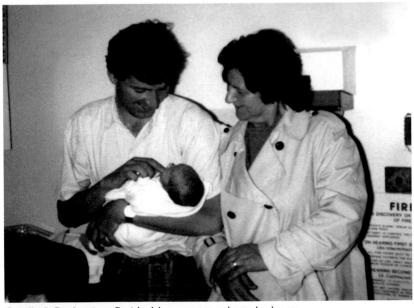

Cradled: Dad gets a first hold as my proud nan looks on

Born a Red:
Aged four months
and already wearing
my colours

Thumbs up: A family day out in West Kirby with twin cousins Joseph and Paul

Entertainer: Enjoying a strongman act while holidaying in Bulgaria aged four

Feast: Sampling the cuisine during my first visit to Bulgaria

Travels: Taking in the delights of Turkey during our holiday in Marmaris

Med Red: Showing my Liverpool allegiance abroad, this time in Majorca

All smiles: Seeing in the New Year at Butlins, Skegness, aged 11

Kids' club: Back in Benidorm with my cousins

In control: Taking it easy at home with the television remote

Service: More holiday fun with my cousins in Zante, Greece

My gang: Magaluf with Laura, cousins Becky and Natalie and best mate Lewis

Taking the mic: Hitting the karaoke alongside a holidaymaker with poor taste!

Sister act: Dressed up to celebrate Laura's 21st birthday with Melissa

The oldest of them would nod at me now and again and say, "Liverpool" or "Steven Gerrard" and once he did the Dudek legs. About two hours later he was taken away and I sat on his empty bed. It was rock solid. Like laying on concrete; a few old sheets were cast over it and a manky, stained pillow.

The fellas in my cell were OK. One tall and skinny, the other puny with a funny, puffed-out chest and slight hunch in his back.

I used to lie there sometimes in the dark, maybe until about 3am, going through everything in my mind. What if I'd done this? What if I'd done that? Just running through all the alternatives to the situation I was in. I wanted to be at home celebrating with my dad, not here.

I would pray it was all one big, horrific mistake and that it'd soon be sorted. I just wanted to hear the key in that door and be told I could go home. But every time the door opened, it was only to cuff me and take me to see an investigator.

They told me it was a very serious crime and asked me what happened.

I repeated it again: "I wasn't there. I don't know what happened. Is my dad here?"

Instead of answering me, I was taken back up to the cells. Two days later they came into my cell again and said I was going to court. I was cuffed to Anthony Wilson and the two of us were shoved into a stinking van with two other prisoners inside already.

"Bradley's got bail lad," said Anthony. "He's out already. Hope that means we get it."

After a short journey, the van pulled up outside the court and when the doors were slid open, a barrage of flashlights went off in our faces.

Instinctively, we both tried to hide our faces as we were led in. After a short wait in a holding cell, we were taken into the courtroom. Anthony's brother was there and told us to keep our faces covered. The flash bulbs were still snapping away and I could see a TV camera crew from the corner of my eye.

Sat in the row before Anthony's brother was a girl who I could tell instantly was a Scouser. I didn't recognise her, but she told us it was going to be OK and that my dad would be in Varna that night.

Anthony went up first. I watched intently and as the translator explained what the judge was saying, he suddenly slumped and started to cry. My head was whirring. What were they saying that had upset him so much?

He came back over, snivelling a little and wiping his eyes.

"I'm going down for 10 to 15 years lad," he said in disbelief. "10 to fucking 15."

It was my turn next and the translator, a dour woman wearing big Deirdre Barlow glasses, told me I wouldn't be getting bail and they had enough evidence to jail me for 15 to 20 years.

Time seemed to slow down. My blood ran cold and my ears stopped working suddenly. It was as if I blacked out although I was stood there straight. It was all happening so quickly.

Feeling numb, we covered our faces as we were led away and I could hear the Scouse girl saying we have got lawyers working on it and that we'd be OK.

The next day I was hoping my dad would be able to come in, but it didn't happen. I could hear someone shouting "Michael" but realised it was Anthony's voice coming from further down the corridor.

There was no sign of my dad over the weekend either but I knew he would be trying to get in to see me. I was allowed out of the room once over the following four days for a shower. I didn't eat anything, instead just drinking water.

The food they gave me was mush. I could hardly look at it and besides, I didn't feel hungry. I just felt sick, constantly sick, and lonely.

THE PHONE CALL WHICH MADE
MY BLOOD RUN COLD
By Michael Shields Senior

The phone rang, it was one of my nephews, Paul Graney.

"Don't panic Mick, but there's been some trouble and the police have taken Michael to be questioned. He wasn't there though."

"What kind of trouble? Why have they taken our Michael?" I asked.

"A Bulgarian waiter has been hit on the head with a stone," he said. "But Michael wasn't there. He was in bed. We've been told he's gone down to the station with another few lads and one of them has been released already. Don't worry about it – he's done nothing wrong."

As the day wore on, we got more and more calls. It became obvious there had been a very serious incident, and this waiter had been very seriously hurt.

By now, some of the family had come around to see how they could help. One of Maria's brothers phoned the British embassy to try and fathom out what was going on.

"I'm phoning about my nephew, Michael Shields," he said. "He's been arrested in Varna. We'd like to know what for."

"Michael hasn't been arrested," said the embassy staffer. "We can't tell you the name of who has been arrested, but Michael hasn't. We can reassure you of that. "

Then I got a phone call on my mobile which made my blood run cold.

"Michael you better get over here," he said. "Your lad has been picked out of an identity parade for attempted murder."

I lost it. The embassy had been saying he hadn't been arrested, and then my mate was saying he'd been picked from an ID parade. What was going on? I was frantic.

I started looking for flights hurriedly and quickly booked one along with two of Michael's uncles. We'd been told Michael could be kept for up to 72 days without being charged under Bulgarian law, and there was no way we were leaving him on his own.

When we got there, I booked into the hotel Michael had been staying in. I wanted to suss it out for myself and see what people were saying.

It was a brand new hotel, but when I asked the staff if the CCTV cameras over the door were working, they said they were broken. Those cameras could've shown Michael walking into the lobby hours before the attack.

I was starting to worry more and more about Michael's safety. What if he got attacked in prison by someone thinking he'd dropped a stone on that man's head? One of their own had been hurt. Surely the Bulgarian prisoners wouldn't look kindly on him.

In hindsight, I shouldn't have stayed at the hotel where Michael had been. We didn't seem welcome. Although we didn't go around broadcasting who we were, the hotel staff obviously knew.

In Varna, it seemed like all anybody was interested in was your money. There were prostitutes and pimps standing around in the middle of the resort at night and everyone wanted to rip you off. It didn't feel safe.

I made good friends with a couple called Julie and John from Merseyside who were having a holiday in Golden Sands, the resort just outside Varna where Michael had been staying.

At first I didn't tell them who I was or why I was there but eventually I confided in them. Michael's uncles had to return home by then and I was alone. Julie and John were fantastic and didn't leave my side after that.

They kept me company and kept my mind occupied in between visiting Michael and trying to do what I could.

Then one afternoon I was called to the hotel reception.

"Mr Shields you are going to have to vacate your room," said the young lady. "The hotel is all booked up."

It seemed like a lame excuse. They just didn't want me there anymore – but I was happy to get away. I went and booked a different hotel straight away.

I was woken up on Monday morning by the latch going on the door. A policeman walked in and spoke to one of my cellmates. The cellmate flashed 10 fingers at me.

Thinking he meant 10 minutes, I hurriedly started to get washed and dressed. But 10 minutes came and went, as did 20, and then what felt like an hour. He'd meant 10am.

Eventually the door opened again and the same routine as last week unravelled. I was cuffed to Anthony and we were pushed into a van, barely big enough for four, with six lads in it.

It was hotter than usual and the smell made me balk. At the court, we jumped out and covered our faces again as the flashlights went off.

I was trying to figure out why we were back there and Anthony, who seemed a bit more clued up, told me it was a bail appeal. As we walked into court, I saw my dad standing there. It was the first time I'd seen him since all this happened and I felt happy and overwhelmed all at once. All of a sudden, my legs felt like jelly and I started to sob.

Dad leaned across and touched my head: "Keep your head up Michael," he said. "Keep your head up son. There are loads of witnesses for you. It's going to be alright."

Anthony and I were led to the front of the court. I was still sobbing. Obviously I'd never cry in public, I could barely remember crying since I was a little kid, but I didn't care.

A middle-aged man with wavy grey hair sat next to me and introduced himself as my lawyer.

"This will not take long," he said, smiling.

I noticed my dad had bags with him. Even if I didn't get bail, I knew he'd be around and would come to see me.

This time I was up first and it was similar to the last hearing, except now they were talking about possible sentences of life and life with no parole.

Through my sobs I heard the translator say there would be no bail and no further appeals.

I watched my dad as we were led out and his eyes were filling up. It brought back my tears.

"Stay strong Michael," he was shouting, his face red. He looked tired. "Stay strong – you've done nothing wrong. We'll sort this out."

It looked like Anthony might have got bail. His lawyers were talking far longer than mine. But the outcome was that he couldn't, and we were cuffed together again.

My dad ran over as we were led away from court.

"I'm coming to see you later," he said. "It's going to be OK. Try and eat something lad. We're going to sort this out."

He was spitting his words out, trying to say as much as he could before I was put into the van again.

Back at the detention centre, I had been in the cell for an hour when the door opened and I was taken downstairs in cuffs.

I was ushered into the investigation room where I'd been before. Dad was sat there. He jumped up and hugged me as my hands were getting uncuffed.

He explained that everyone I'd been on holiday with had come to our house and told him what had happened. They'd said I hadn't been involved and that I'd been in bed. I began to feel good for the first time in weeks.

"We're having a meeting with a new lawyer," he said. "There's letters here from your mum and our Melissa and Laura."

The room was tiny and crumbling. We were being watched by an investigator and an officer, too. He was only allowed in for 20 minutes. Dad wasn't allowed to give me anything, so he had to read the letters to me.

It was very difficult. These two Bulgarian fellas just sat there, one listening and the other translating what dad was reading.

Dad was doing his best not to cry, but I couldn't help it. I was crying my eyes out as he read, thinking about my mum's face and how upset she must have been about this.

Dad had brought some food and drinks for me. He also had a quilt with a pillow. We only got 15 minutes together, but it was special. Just being with him gave me strength.

As he left, we hugged each other again and he ruffled my hair, which was cropped short. I'd stopped crying.

Afterwards, a woman from the British embassy came in and asked me how I was. I recognised her face from court. I asked for some paper and a pen and she promised to bring some as she left. I went back to my cell feeling stronger, remembering what my dad said.

LEAFLETS FLOOD CITY IN SUPPORT OF JAILED REDS FAN SHIELDS
By Greg O'Keeffe

THOUSANDS of leaflets and posters calling for the release of jailed teenager Michael Shields were today distributed across Liverpool.

The 18-year-old engineering student spent his 10th night in a Bulgarian prison yesterday, accused of attempted murder.

His family hope the leaflets will prompt Reds fans who witnessed the alleged assault to come forward and clear Mr Shields' name.

He was travelling home from Liverpool's Champions League triumph in Istanbul when he was arrested for throwing a stone at a Bulgarian man.

Friends and guests at the Kristal hotel where Mr Shields stayed say he was in bed at the time of the alleged assault.

Two other Liverpool fans were accused in connection with the incident.

Bradley Thompson, 19, was released on bail earlier this week but must remain in Bulgaria for 30 days.

Anthony Wilson, 18, is in custody.

– Liverpool Echo, June 10, 2005

6. In a Bulgarian Jail

Back in my cell, I started to look through what was in the bag dad handed me. There was a Game Boy and he'd put an A4 pad in, too. I wrote a few letters to my mum and the girls to fill time, and then played on the Game Boy until the batteries began to fade.

I still wasn't feeling hungry and knew I'd lost weight. I tried to distract myself any way possible during the day. The radio was on constantly, but I didn't understand a word the DJ said. Now and then I'd recognise the odd song, but otherwise it was just background noise.

At night we were allowed to watch a TV which was marginally bigger than the palm of my hand. I gave up watching after a while and started to write down what had happened to me. I wanted to get as much of my experience as possible down on paper. I'd never kept a diary before but it felt good to get my thoughts down on paper.

A few days came and went until my dad came to see me again, this time with my uncle Joey and another new lawyer. I had to sign more papers confirming that this new fella could represent me.

I managed to keep myself together and my dad gave me another plastic bag with crisps and bottles of Coke in. He'd brought one for Anthony as well.

The lawyer had a list with him which had Kieran, John and Geoff's names and addresses on it. He was saying to my dad that he wanted them out here by the following Wednesday, but as far as I knew, the next court hearing wasn't for three weeks.

I began to pray that maybe something had changed for the good.

HEARTBREAKING LETTERS FROM HIS JAIL CELL
Exclusive By Greg O'Keeffe

THE inner turmoil of jailed Reds fan Michael Shields is revealed today in heartbreaking letters from his Bulgarian prison cell.

In an emotional letter to his mother Maria, and an open letter to all his friends back in Liverpool, the teenager's fear and bewilderment are clear to see.

The 18-year-old was arrested after being seized in a Bulgarian hotel as he returned from Liverpool FC's victory in Istanbul.

He remains locked up for a crime he insists he did not commit, without any charges being brought.

With his health deteriorating, Michael has made a public plea for help.

ALL I WANT IS MY LIFE BACK
Michael's letters from a cell in Bulgaria

Mum, what started off as one of the best parts of my life has turned out to be so bad... but knowing that my family will be there when the truth comes out and coming home to the greatest city in the world is what's driving me on.

I cannot put into words how much I am missing you. I am counting the days until I can show you. Don't worry yourself over me because all I want is my life back and my family in good health.

The truth will come out but the most satisfying moment was you already knowing I was innocent. I would not do this to my worst enemy.

The people I'm in here with are really nice even though they can't speak English.

They are always cleaning the cell and telling me to get washed. I'm sitting here dreaming of when I get back and you are coming home at 11am from work and shouting me to get up.

Please be strong and keep that scouse cooking for me.

YOU'LL NEVER WALK ALONE (I will walk every step with you). A big thank you to all the people in Liverpool.

Love, Michael

To Everyone, thanks for all of your support, it's cheering me up when I feel down. I still cannot believe there is a campaign and people are walking around with my face on their T-shirts.

There is no day I am looking forward to more than the day I come home. I've just finished the letters and I was crying, but it was not a sad cry – it was a happy cry.

I know how fortunate I am to have such a wonderful family supporting me. I sleep with my letters under my pillow and I will keep going strong. I am just looking forward to the day I am home.

To my nephew and niece (Philip, 4, and Kelsey, 9): Don't get too comfortable with the remote, with my computer, or in my bed – but keep it warm.

Love, Michael
– Liverpool Echo, June 27, 2005

When I got back to my cell, one of the fellas I'd got to know was gone. I was already getting used to the chopping and changing all the time. It was a shame because I liked him. He would often be allowed out, I never found out why, and would come back and tell me I was in the newspapers and on the TV.

I found out from Anthony that he'd seen a newspaper which

had a story about us on the front page, with a big photograph of us going into court.

That night another new person came into the cell. He recognised me immediately and could speak English. I was made up – it was someone to talk to. He asked me if I was guilty and I explained to him what had happened.

"Why are you in here?" I asked, pleased that he seemed to believe me.

He said he had been mistaken for someone who had been taking money from banks using fake ID. We got talking about the differences between Bulgaria and England. The prices of things like cars and houses.

"Money rules in Bulgaria," he said. "Money is number one. If you pay the person who gets hurt, then you go home."

It made me think. But why should I pay someone who I've done nothing to? I want to prove to people here that I haven't done anything wrong. He started to tell me he could get in touch with the waiter who was hurt if I wanted, but I told him that I'd be free as soon as the truth got out.

The days passed. I completed Super Mario on the Game Boy and learned to play a new card game. I was praying constantly that the lawyer was getting my defence together. I began to feel more confident of going home.

The embassy delivered some books I'd asked for along with some bottles of water. I'd started reading a whole book in a day. While I was laying on my bed reading, the guards pushed someone else into our cell.

Four people in a three-bed cell.

The new fella was given a mattress and told to sleep on the floor. The next day he had to be moved because he was in agony from cramps.

My thoughts rarely strayed from my case and proving I was

innocent. When I slept, I dreamed of home and when I woke so far from that place, I felt sad. Even if I lay down to doze during the day, home would creep into my mind. I just wanted to wake up in my normal bed.

I had only seen my dad twice since I'd been in Varna detention centre. The first time had been a very quick visit because he had to go and see my lawyer. I knew I was only allowed two family visits a month, but I was wondering why my lawyer hadn't been in more often. They were allowed to come in far more than family.

I was already on my third book and getting bored of every possible card game you could imagine.

One morning, the anxiety about not seeing my lawyer was building up to a head. Then the door opened and I was told to come out.

Finally, I was going to meet my lawyer – or 'advocat' in Bulgarian. But would my dad be there?

Inside the room, a translator was sitting next to a big, fierce-looking blonde woman. She is one of the main investigators. I asked my lawyer if I could see my dad and he said probably not.

He explained that dad was downstairs with my witnesses. My lawyer then asked me to go through everything I did on that night. So I went through it, slowly and calmly. Then when we'd finished, he read me the prosecution's final statement. It was crap – saying I was a hooligan and I'd tried to kill someone.

"I'M NOT GUILTY," I said, trying not to shout. "I haven't done what they're saying."

The lawyer told me I would be going back to court tomorrow for another ID parade. I thought I should be pleased with that, but remembering what a shambles the first one was, I became paranoid.

Before I was ushered back up to my cell, I told the lawyer to get me more meetings with my dad.

It turned out the second ID parade was to be held at the detention centre and not in court. I had been told the other lads would at least look like me this time, but again they didn't. As we stood there, people looked through a little window and I could hear them talking.

As they spoke, the investigator was typing. The translator, who was also in the room, said I had been picked out and that my lawyer was objecting.

He said that I had been noticed because of my blond hair. I was the only person in the line-up with blond hair. The other three had dark hair and were darker skinned.

Suddenly, the waiter who had been attacked walked into the room. He took off his hat and pointed to the nasty, jagged wound on his skull with rows of jet-black staples in it.

I tried to tell him I was sorry for his injuries but he must have known it wasn't me. I was frantically trying to get his attention but he went after a moment. I felt sick.

Again I asked my lawyer if my dad was there. He wasn't, but my uncle Jimmy was. He explained that Jimmy would be able to come in and see me the next day.

The lawyer explained that the police case was fully closed and all their evidence was now ready for the trial. He said it meant I would be allowed more visits – maybe one a week.

Back in the cell I played a new card game called Svard which I had learned from my English-speaking mate. I was lucky he was there because he helped me communicate with a lot of the others.

One night particularly sticks in my mind from that time. I was just dozing off and I heard this horrible screaming from what sounded like a woman.

I tried to wake my cellmate up, but he just waved me off and turned back over saying it was a drunk gypsy woman they'd brought in. I couldn't get the sound of her screaming out of my head. She was getting beaten up badly and it took what seemed like ages. I wanted to do something but I couldn't. I didn't sleep much that night.

It amazed me how I slept at all in that place but I suppose your body just adjusts. I certainly had to adjust to some pretty grim things. Another night not long after I got to the detention centre I was starting to drift off. It was just after lights out and the cell was quiet except for the other prisoners' snoring.

Suddenly I felt things start to fall onto me from the ceiling. I hunched down into my thin blanket and tried to cover myself thinking it was a heavy drip, but it got heavier and heavier. I sunk lower and lower into the sheet until only the top of my head was sticking out, but felt more things fall on me. Then they started to move.

I reached for a book and started to whack at them wildly, panic building up inside. Then it stopped. After half an hour of laying there wide awake, nothing more fell on me. Somehow I fell asleep. It wasn't as if I could flick a light on to check what it was.

I awoke the next morning to find my sheets splattered with the blood of several huge cockroaches. The remains of the ugly black creatures, one of them the size of my hand, were all over my bed. I gagged. The other lads in the cell said they had often felt them crawling over them.

'That's it. I'll never sleep again,' I thought. But I did. Even though the cockroaches came back from time to time, I managed to sleep. It is amazing how you cope with things.

My dreams of home were getting more and more realistic. Each time I'd wake up feeling more sad and lonely. Sometimes I could barely believe I was in a cell when I woke up, the dreams were that vivid.

Jimmy didn't come in the next day and there was no sign of the lawyer either.

I managed to ask a guard, through my cellmate, if I could swap books with Anthony. Anything to get me through the next few days.

I was desperate to see my dad. I couldn't shake off the image of that lad's head. It was clear it was very serious, but I didn't hurt him.

Sunday came and I was expecting yet another day of boredom, until the door opened at 11am. I was taken to see my lawyer again and noticed a blue envelope on the table of the interview room. The translator said they were letters from home. They added that dad was there and I could see him later on.

Before that, though, they read some witness statements to me. Three people had positively identified me as being the person who attacked the waiter.

They said I had been wearing a white T-shirt when it happened at 5.30am. My head began to spin. I had been wearing a beige T-shirt and had been in bed at 2.30am.

The statements all seemed to say the same thing. A fat boy with blond hair had dropped a big stone on the waiter's head. My lawyer said everyone had signed their statement saying it was the truth.

There were other statements from strangers, but others from people I knew like Spud and Powelly. Other lads from the hotel had also come forward, but I couldn't see Geoff's name and it puzzled me.

With my stack of letters in my hand, I was sent back to the cell to wait until 3pm to see my dad. In my cell, I began to read my letters, including one from my cousins Kenny, Ashley and Stephen, which said there was a banner outside my house which said 'MICHAEL IS INNOCENT'.

Apparently someone had knocked at ours and said it was nice that they were supporting Michael Jackson. I let out a rare laugh.

There was one from my little niece, Kelsey, saying that she had been thrown from house to house but now she was back home.

The one from our Laura said there were girls who didn't know me wearing T-shirts with my name on, so there was no reason for me not to get a girlfriend now. She said someone had asked my little nephew Philip if he wanted me home and he'd said no because I wouldn't let him on the computer. Again, I chuckled.

Our Melissa said she had been getting stopped in the street by people who knew she was my sister, and that her and my Aunty Lillian had just got back from the Radio City tower.

There were 6,000 posters saying I was innocent across the city, too. It really gave me a lift, and when I went to see my dad I tried to stay strong.

SUPPORT FOR FAN IN JAIL
By Greg O'Keeffe

THE plight of jailed Reds fan Michael Shields was highlighted as his team played TNS in the European Cup qualifying match.

Many fans held giant banners calling for the 18-year-old to be freed from his Bulgarian prison, and wore T-shirts with his face printed on them.

The banners were seen by millions of TV viewers across the world and Liverpool FC have also backed the campaign on their website.

Members of Michael's family were at the game against the Welsh side, handing out leaflets about the student, whose trial for attempted murder in Bulgaria is only a week away.

He is currently on remand at a prison in Varna awaiting a trial next week and could face a 20-year jail term if convicted.

The Kop season-ticket holder, from Wavertree, was arrested in *the Bulgarian resort of Golden Sands as he travelled home from watching Liverpool's Champions League final triumph in Istanbul in May.*

He was arrested alongside two other Liverpool youths, and accused of hitting a Bulgarian bartender over the head with a slate and leaving him for dead.

But Michael, who insists he was in bed at his hotel when the attack happened, has been backed by several independent witnesses who say he was with them.

The Echo has revealed how Michael was forced to take part in an identity parade in clothes he was not wearing on the night of the attack. And Wavertree MP Louise Ellman has written to Tony Blair calling for Michael's case to be reviewed before trial.

– Liverpool Echo, July 14, 2005

Dad said the campaign was good and that I should stay strong. The translator said that if I started to cry, the meeting would be stopped.

Dad was insisting I'd get out, even if it went to a trial. Shortly, the blonde investigator called the meeting over and said there was someone from the British Consul to see me.

It was another translator, this time a Cockney woman, and she asked what I needed. I told her I'd finished all my books and could she get me more books, magazines and English newspapers. Then she left to see Anthony.

Knowing I had all that support helped me to sleep a bit easier. I'd been given an English-to-Bulgarian phrase book and tried to have a laugh with my cellmates by playing daft tricks on the guards.

I was hoping the embassy could get me more stuff to read, and I never stopped praying I'd get bail, although I knew it was very unlikely. I kept wondering whether the people who had signed those statements identifying me knew they were wrong. Were they lying for some reason? I would have to prove them wrong.

Over the next couple of days I started to do some press-ups and sit-ups. At first I couldn't do many but each time I tried, I'd be able to squeeze out one more press-up. My arms ached and shook, but it felt good.

Then, for the first time since I'd been in the detention centre, I was allowed into a big room with windows on the top floor to do some exercise. There was nothing to do except jump up and try to look outside. Try to breathe in the fresh air. I must have looked pretty stupid just bouncing around that room, jumping up and trying to see the sky. I felt silly too, but at the same time, I enjoyed it and hoped I'd be allowed back. I'd only been in there for 15 minutes but I was out of breath. I'd have to get fitter, I thought. Be physically strong as well as in my mind.

I remember the last time my dad came in to see me in the detention centre.

"You're going to the adult prison soon," he said. "We've got you a new lawyer and he's getting you moved."

LONG WAY FROM HOME, IS IT LOOKING GOOD?
By Greg O'Keeffe, in Varna, Bulgaria

THROUGH a window the size of a cat-flap, the guard collects our passports and tells us to wait. It is 30C and the next visiting time at the Varna jailhouse is not for half an hour.

Michael Shields Snr smokes incessantly and broods in the heat.

Today, for the first time, he has seen the place his son will spend the next three weeks.

Around him the sombre grounds of the jail defy the sunshine. Barbed wire covers the exterior and guards patrol in military-style jumpsuits and caps.

Stray dogs lounge in the shade and only the noise of traffic from the busy suburban street punctuates the silence.

Nobody knows what to say.

"Get your head up lad," says Michael's brother-in-law Jimmy. "He needs to see us being strong for him."

For Michael Shields Snr this is the last place on earth his son should be. The tall iron doors to the building open and a dozen local visitors file out.

Some are girlfriends pushing prams, others doleful parents, others siblings. A woman carrying a toddler cannot stop the tears rolling down her face.

When it is time, a guard leads us inside and across a dusty courtyard. We take a flight of stairs to the first floor where the new prisoners are held and that is where Michael Shields, head freshly shaved, is waiting.

Michael, 6ft, with wide shoulders and an open face, is wearing a red designer T-shirt and tracksuit bottoms. Despite his size, he barely looks 18, and he wears a brace on his teeth. He hugs his father and for a moment battles the onset of tears.

Gradually, over the next 40 minutes the colour returns to Michael's face as he chats to his father and uncle.

"Who have we (Liverpool) signed, dad?" asks Michael, beaming at the news his Anfield season-ticket waits at home for him. "I keep thinking about getting home and going the match. I phoned my nan yesterday.

"I'm sleeping OK now. They wake us up at six, but once they have checked the cells, I can get back to sleep. The noise of the others doesn't bother me as much anymore – it's just the heat.

"How are things looking? Is it looking good?" With little notice, time is up.

After a minute spent alone, Michael Snr emerges from the room with his son in tow. We are led one way, Michael Shields, flanked by guards, the other.

As he reaches the corridor's end, Michael looks over his shoulder and gives a shy wave.

Suddenly, I didn't want to leave. That stinking, rotten horrible place had actually become home. In a way, I'd got comfortable. That was the same story all the time after that. I'd just adjust to one prison and then it'd be time to move on. Suddenly I'd have to swap somewhere I'd managed to survive and sussed out for a new place full of new risks and unknowns.

I'd be thinking, I won't last in this new place. There is no way to survive. I was thinking: "I can't hack this."

We arrived at the adult prison and the first person I met was this big guy with dark hair who spoke a bit of English. He was in his own clothes and seemed very relaxed. I thought he was one of the main men or something then I realised he was actually a prisoner, too. This was Ivan. Ivan was the unofficial induction officer, charged with looking after new prisoners. We would become good friends. I was still there with Anthony Wilson, one of the other Scouse lads who got arrested.

We went through two sets of gates into this place which was a bit like a POW camp from the films with an open courtyard and guards with guns and caps walking round everywhere. We walked into the main room and there were some prisoners eating dinner, and we were walked past others who were still in cells, and this one fella had a cutlery knife in his hand and he was staring at us and rattling it across the bars. He was doing it really slowly and deliberately. Just staring at us with this intimidating expression on his face. I couldn't stop seeing him doing that with the knife and thinking he was going to cut us up.

SHIELDS' PRISON HELL — I'M SCARED THE TRUTH WON'T COME OUT
Exclusive By Greg O'Keeffe, in Varna, Bulgaria

JAILED Liverpool teenager Michael Shields today spoke of his nightmare behind bars, accused of a crime he insists he did not commit.

In an exclusive interview in his Bulgarian cell, the 18-year-old described his life in a foreign prison as he awaits trial for attempted murder.

Fighting back tears, he said: "I'm scared the truth won't come out. I can't describe how sick the frustration makes me feel."

The Edge Hill student was arrested in May as he holidayed at the Golden Sands Resort near Varna, after travelling to Istanbul to watch Liverpool FC's victory in the Champions League.

He is accused of attacking a 25-year-old Bulgarian man and leaving him for dead.

Today Mr Shields revealed:
* Police left him handcuffed to a radiator alone for a whole night after his arrest.
* He was forced to wear clothes in an identity parade he did not wear on the night of the assault.
* Officers grilled him until he broke down and pleaded for his father.
* The results of an alcohol and blood test he took were negative.

Mr Shields was arrested with two other Merseysiders and held for a month in a police jail without charge while his family tried to get him freed.

Last week he was formally charged – his trial is due later this month – even though several witnesses signed statements saying that he was asleep in his hotel room at the time of the attack.

Recalling the night of May 29, Mr Shields said: "The police

*kept saying there had been a fight and someone had battered
a Bulgarian man.*

"I didn't see much trouble in Bulgaria. The only grief was in
Muppets bar when a Scouser and a German bloke were
fighting over a comment said to the German's girlfriend.

"They took me to the police station in Golden Sands and
handcuffed me to a radiator. I was there for about four hours
until the rep from our hotel came with food.

"After that they handcuffed me to the radiator again and left
me there for the rest of that afternoon and night.

"I was terrified and my mind was racing. I kept saying to
them that I didn't know the two lads I'd been arrested with."

*After a sleepless night, Mr Shields was made to take part in
an identity parade the next day.*

"They made me wear a white T-shirt because the attacker
wore one, but I had a beige T-shirt and black shorts on that
night," he said.

"When I got picked from the first one I felt sick. There was
another parade and all the other guys were a lot older and very
dark-skinned. They all had jumpers on and I still had this white
T-shirt.

"I said it wasn't fair and I asked for a jumper as well. I must
have got picked again because after that I was interviewed by
their detectives.

"They kept asking me what happened that night, over and
over again. I was sick of saying I wasn't even there so
eventually I refused to go on until I spoke to my dad or a
solicitor."

*Last week after being formally charged, Mr Shields was
moved to a new jail in a Varna suburb. He was refused bail and
must wait for a trial on July 21.*

He said: "I try and break up the day by learning Bulgarian
from a phrase book and sometimes I do press-ups. Yesterday
they shaved my head because it's so hot."

*A brace fixed to Mr Shields' teeth was due to be removed a
month ago.*

"My mouth is always sore but I haven't seen a dentist. I can't

eat the jail food so I just eat what dad brings me," he added.
"I get sad and I'm worried about my family but I'm trying to
be strong. My dad tells me to keep my head up."
– Liverpool Echo, July 7, 2005

Then Ivan led me to what was going to be our cell, and to my surprise and relief it was a small, clean room.

There was a shower and some stuff like a towel and soap on the bed. We were hungry when we got in so we had a Pot Noodle which my dad had given me and we realised there was even a little room with an old TV in which worked.

After we'd finally had some food, Ivan introduced me to Chuska (a nickname meaning 'pepper' in Bulgarian), who was in charge of keeping the cells tidy. Everyone had his own little job in there and Ivan told him what to do.

Chuska was a small, stocky young lad with a shaved head. He definitely wasn't the sharpest tool in the box.

He was in there because one day his baby had been crying and he'd lost his temper and hit her. It'd killed the baby.

Despite that, he wasn't evil like you'd imagine a child killer to be. He seemed basically nice.

I got a big shock when I finally found out why Ivan was in, too. He'd murdered someone.

On the outside, if someone tells you that they'd taken another person's life, you'd think: 'That must be one evil person', but it's not always that simple. Ivan had a kind, calm presence and put himself out for people.

Some of the lads I came across later, in English prisons like Garth, I might have thought: 'You deserve to be locked away. You're an animal.' But Ivan wasn't like that.

He helped me adjust to the new jail, and by June I was thinking: 'If I can just get through to the trial, I'll be OK.' It didn't cross my mind that I'd be found guilty. I thought I'd be out when the truth came out.

But then after that, after a year-and-a-half in Bulgaria, I was just thinking: 'I need to get out of here. It doesn't matter how. I need to leave this country.'

7. The Trial

It had got to the stage when every time I heard something, it was bad news. After a visit I would be happy, but then I'd hear my name mentioned by the newsreader on the tiny TV set in our cell or I'd catch a glimpse of a newspaper with my photograph in it.

It wasn't a surprise they had so many pictures. I was amazed at the amount of cameras from the moment I went to court for the first bail hearing. That was when the severity of the upcoming trial really dawned on me.

It was me and Wilson at that hearing. He went in first and then came back crying.

"They've just told me I'm getting 15 years," he said, tears streaming down his face.

Those now familiar knots tightened in my stomach again. They called me up and I walked into the court. A translator stood beside me whispering everything that was being said by the judge to me. There was a prosecuting lawyer there too and my unease got even stronger when I kept hearing them mentioning "articles" and the words "20 years" and "25 years", then the translator was whispering about "life" and "life without parole" and I could feel the blood draining from my face. I must have been white.

Again I was thinking: 'Am I really standing here? Is this really happening?' I trooped back outside to where Wilson was and said, half-joking: "I think I've just got lucky. I don't know what happened but I definitely heard life – with parole."

Neither of us knew at the time that they had simply been discussing possible maximum sentences for our so-called crimes if we were convicted. They had to go through the relevant laws when they were deciding on bail.

We were put back in the van and driven back to the detention centre. As the van trundled along the road we were saying to the guards "solicitor" and "lawyer", trying to get a reassurance we could see one any time soon. They just looked at us and didn't answer. One pointed to his ear and shrugged.

It was only later that I learned the Bulgarian for lawyer is 'advokat'. It was only after being back in my cell for two hours of clumsy conversation that my pad-mates worked out it was only a bail hearing. I hadn't just been sentenced to life with parole after all.

The following evening a guard came into my pad and said the trial was going to start the next day and I had to be up and ready at 7.30am.

Another predictably long night followed, catching half-hours of sleep here and there, my mind whirring. By the time morning came, I'd gone over every possibility of what could happen.

The first thing I didn't like about that day was what I had to wear. My dad had sorted me out a smart shirt and some black pants. I felt uncomfortable in them and wanted to wear my jeans and a shirt. As I was preparing myself, I was talking to my pad-mates a bit – desperately searching for some hope to cling on to.

It'd always been like that since the start. If someone said: "You're only 18, they won't be hard on you", I'd get my hopes up. Other times, though, they'd say: "You've hurt a Bulgarian. You'll probably go away for a long time."

We got the shout to leave our cells and head to the van. As I got outside into the sunlight, I saw the usual rickety van waiting to take us. It absolutely stunk. There was room inside for four people at a push but there were six of us crammed inside. I gagged when they shut the doors, trying not to vomit at the stench.

Anthony was squeezed in one corner and I was in another, with a guard either side of us. On previous court visits we'd been dropped off behind the building, but on that day we were dropped off at a different spot. We were marched to a smaller court room, which seemed to be opposite the main court where the trial was going to take place.

We could both hear the build-up to the trial from the other court, the stern voices and the overlapping as one lawyer interrupted another.

Wilson and I chatted quietly, trying to get some hope out of each other.

"They can't do me for this surely?" I said.

"I can't go down for a little bit of weed can I?" he replied.

We both said what we wanted to hear to each other, but deep down I'd started to lose faith in things all turning out OK.

My lawyer, Borislav Shislovsky, walked into the smaller court. The tension was the most I've ever felt. Straight away I saw he was a ringer for Rick Astley and allowed myself a little laugh. It was time to go in, he said. He led the way and that's when I saw all the different photographers and people everywhere.

As ever, I scanned the courtroom for a friendly face and saw my dad and sisters sitting looking nervous among all the Bulgarian court officials. I smiled at them as we were led to a table roughly opposite where the judge was sitting.

As we were told where to stand, another door opened and all the photographers and TV news cameras were suddenly allowed into the room. Instinctively I put my head down, trying to avoid the glare and the flashing cameras. I looked at my dad but he motioned for me to lift it up.

"Get your head up," he said.

"You've got no reason to hide your face, Michael.

"Keep your head up."

'HOLD YOUR HEAD UP MICHAEL, YOU HAVE GOT NOTHING TO BE ASHAMED OF, SON'
By Greg O'Keeffe

WATCHING his son shuffle dejectedly from court with his head bowed was too much for Michael Shields's father to take.

After a day when tensions had run even higher than the temperature in the tiny Varna courtroom, it was the final straw.

"Hold your head up Michael, you've got nothing to be ashamed of," shouted Michael Snr.

The outburst was not only an instruction to his shell-shocked son, it was a declaration to the assortment of media, witnesses and officials gathered for the first day of this attempted murder trial.

Wavertree engineering student Shields left the court flanked by armed guards. He had been banned from speaking to the five members of his family present.

Shields, 18, has always denied the attack which the court learned left an innocent barman in a coma. His family and legal team will hope to convince the jury that his arrest was a case of mistaken identity.

But his world must have stopped turning when barmaid Daniella Krumova, 20, stood before the court and insisted he was responsible.

Ms Krumova had no doubt that Shields had been the person who subjected barman Martin Georgiev to the final sickening blow in an attack of sustained savagery.

The words "with such force that it bounced off his head" must have echoed around the silent court.

Back home in Liverpool, other members of the Shields family were spared the gruesome details of the prosecution opening statement, but they endured their own form of torture.

"We've been waiting for the phone to ring all day but it hasn't," said his older sister Melissa.

"The tension has been very hard. His future is being decided over there and there's nothing we can do.

"I saw Michael's photo in the Echo yesterday but I couldn't

> *read what they say he did. I know my brother isn't capable of*
> *hurting anyone.*
>
> *"That picture on the front page was the first time I've seen*
> *Michael in over a month.*
>
> *"In a weird way I was pleased with how well he looked*
> *because I've been dreading seeing him.*
>
> *"But imagining what he is going through is too hard.*
>
> *"I know there are witnesses who say it was Michael but the*
> *defence has witnesses who say it wasn't. I just hope they believe*
> *our side."*
>
> *– Liverpool Echo, July 22, 2005*

We both sat down then and Wilson immediately buried his face in his hands, but I put my shoulders back and my chest out. After five minutes of preamble, the translator asked if I wanted the media there, and I said no. I was uneasy enough without the constant flashing and the cameras trained on me.

Glancing around the room, I suddenly realised that just a couple of yards from me was Martin Georgiev, the man who'd been attacked. He was so close.

I was thinking: 'How can he be allowed to sit so close to me if I'm supposed to have hurt him so badly?' I began to try and make eye contact with him. Every time he would look in my direction, I'd desperately try to get him to meet my gaze. I had a flashback to the second ID parade, seeing him, and when he pointed to his head and said in perfect English:

"Look what you've done to me."

I decided to try and speak to him amid the clatter of the court.

"You know this is not right," I said. "You know I did not do it to you." But he was looking away and his lawyer was touching his shoulder and seemed to be telling him to ignore me. I felt incensed. I wanted to keep on at him. To grab his attention. How could he ignore me?

He was wearing a hat but quickly took it off to reveal his shaved head and a jagged scar where he'd been injured. It looked nasty. Suddenly I felt sorry for him and realised he was a victim, but at the same time it was nothing to do with me. I still tried to make eye contact but he seemed determined not to.

It all began to feel surreal, the constant chatter in Bulgarian and a translator whispering to me, struggling to keep up. Even her English was a bit faltering and in a heavy accent. I'd be turning to my dad.

"What are they playing at?" I'd say. Or: "This is a joke."

They asked Martin Georgiev in court if he could speak English and he told them he couldn't. Not a word. I was stunned. He'd spoken in perfect English to me at Varna police station during that ID parade. Why was he lying?

It had felt like the longest day of my life. It all seemed to be a blur of people pointing at me, talking about me, accusing me. Finally, though, the first day of the trial had drawn to a close and we were taken back to the detention centre in the revolting van. I was allowed to see my lawyer and he started to go through some witness statements with me. Some of them were describing Wilson and Thompson and then the person I was being mixed up with.

Some said the person who attacked Georgiev had black hair and others said dark hair. Then it had come to the trial and they were all convinced it was me. A lad with fair hair.

Back at court on day two, the case against me continued. I kept hearing that the "English hooligans... did this and then they did that..." Then another statement said: "The fat one threw the brick..." I had to laugh. 'Cheeky bastards,' I thought. 'Who were they calling fat?' Just as I smiled I looked up at the judge, a Bulgarian woman with big hair and glasses. She was staring right at me. 'I better not smile again,' I thought sombrely.

It's a massive understatement to say the Bulgarian court system is different to ours. Two state prosecutors were arguing the case against me, but Martin Georgiev also had two private lawyers who were representing his interests as a victim. I was told they are not strictly supposed to get involved in matters of evidence against the defendant, but they did. Instead of just describing the impact the attack had on their client, they were wading in with stuff about the night of the attack. It felt like I had four prosecutors all gunning for me. My lawyer was getting infuriated because the judge was doing nothing to stop them butting in.

The state prosecutors would say to every witness: "Can you turn around and identify the person who committed the crime?" Each time they would turn around and point at me. The judge didn't question them or query anything about their version of events. Then, when the handful of witnesses for me who'd managed to get over to Bulgaria in time appeared, they were grilled by the judge herself.

One of them was Kevin Glynn, a lad I knew who was in the room below ours at the hotel. He said that during the night of the attack he had climbed up onto the balcony of our room at about 4am and saw me asleep in the room. He said it had been easy to climb up and the lads had been getting up and down between rooms all the time. The Bulgarians didn't believe him. Then, out of nowhere, the judge actually declared it was impossible! How did she know? She had never even been to the hotel.

When I got chances to speak I was telling them I was asleep, but they refused to accept it. They asked me if I'd seen Kevin when he'd climbed up and I said no, because I hadn't. Again, I insisted I was asleep! Then they were asking me how many drinks I'd had? I told them about seven or eight beers, and one of the prosecutors asked if I was an alcoholic.

I explained to them that we'd hardly slept in Istanbul or afterwards in Bulgaria. We'd eaten very little and been up until all hours most nights. I was knackered that night. I was trying to be truthful with them and not lie. I didn't even want to embellish things to make them sound better for me. I hoped if I stuck to the truth, I'd be OK. I tried to say that seven or eight beers made me sleepy. I wasn't a big drinker and I'd gone up to my room because I wanted to rest and save myself for the journey home the following day.

Again Martin Georgiev was saying I had attacked him. He was saying I had punched him and then thrown the brick at him. He even said he didn't even know if Wilson was at the scene of the attack. Each fresh barrage of nonsense had me reeling. I couldn't eat at the lunch breaks. One day Joey brought me a Kentucky Fried Chicken meal to eat and I had to force a few mouthfuls down.

The court sessions lasted some days from 9am until 7pm. By the third day of the trial my dad had flown home because my mum was in a bad way and my uncle Joey was there behind me. They were down to the last dregs of the witnesses by then. A psychiatrist was called up as a prosecution witness and she was saying to the court how surprised she was that I was so relaxed and jovial. If anything, I was a bag of nerves. My whole life was up in the air there, but by then I'd been told that someone had come forward back in Liverpool and was going to admit it was him.

MAN, 20, ADMITS ATTACK ON BULGARIAN BARMAN
World Exclusive By Greg O'Keeffe

AN electrician from Liverpool today dramatically confessed to the attack which has landed teenager Michael Shields in court.

Graham Sankey, from Anfield, admitted he was guilty of the paving slab attack which left a Bulgarian father-of-two in a coma.

Mr Sankey revealed his dark secret after reading about 18-year-old Michael's ongoing trial in the Echo and just weeks after we revealed rumours identifying him as the guilty man.

The 20-year-old broke down in tears as he told top Merseyside solicitor David Kirwan he was the football lout who beat the 25-year-old barman with a paving slab.

He will now accept arrest and prosecution, but will fight any attempts to extradite him to Bulgaria.

Engineering student Michael could now be freed. In a statement, Mr Kirwan said: "Graham Sankey is prepared to admit that he is responsible for the attack in Bulgaria of which Michael Shields stands accused.

"His conscience has told him that he must take these steps to end the agony that Michael and his family have been going through for these past few, horrendous weeks.

"Reading about Michael appearing in a Bulgarian court left him with no alternative but to come forward and admit his part in the events of that night.

"Graham's family, who have received threats themselves in recent days, are standing 100 per cent behind their son even though they are devastated and shattered by what has happened.

"My client is prepared to stand trial only in Britain and to accept the consequences.

"I will be continuing to consider the position very carefully with the Sankey family to ensure that the correct legal processes are observed."

Wavertree teenager Michael Shields was yesterday back before a Bulgarian court in the Black Sea city of Varna standing trial for the attack on Martin Georgiev.

Proceedings were dramatically halted as Mr Sankey was identified in court as the man responsible for the attack. Michael has always insisted he was innocent and his family mounted a two-month campaign to win his freedom.

Legal experts and politicians predict he will now be freed after another man effectively proved his innocence.

– Liverpool Echo, July 23, 2005

FAMILY DELIGHTED AT CHANGE OF HEART
By Greg O'Keeffe

THE family of Michael Shields today revealed their relief at the last-minute confession by electrician Graham Sankey.

Mr Sankey, 20, who had earlier denied the attack which left a Bulgarian barman in a coma, decided to end the Shields' two-month agony by coming forward.

Late yesterday he travelled in secret with his father Edward, a taxi driver, and older brother Dean to consult Merseyside lawyer David Kirwan at his Wirral headquarters.

They thrashed out a statement in which Mr Sankey admitted the attack on 25-year-old Martin Georgiev who had asked a group of Liverpool fans to quieten down as they smashed bottles and chanted outside the bar where he worked.

Yesterday, Michael's family told the Echo they were "delighted" at the development and were looking forward to him being set free and allowed to come home.

The confession was understood to have come after members of Michael's family also made a personal plea to Mr Sankey.

They declined to comment further until Monday when the trial judge is expected to acknowledge the extraordinary twist.

Wavertree MP Louise Ellman, who has also pressed for Michael to be treated fairly and even wrote to foreign secretary Jack Straw about the case, said it was important that the "full truth" had emerged.

Earlier this month Mr Sankey denied the attack in an interview with the Echo. He said then: "I am innocent and I want people to know that."

– Liverpool Echo, July 23, 2005

I was thinking how daft they were all going to look when the truth came out. In the back of my mind I was laughing at them and their charade. The psychiatrist they'd trotted out carried on, saying how I'd shown no remorse. I was being told by my family that once Sankey's confession came through, that would be it. Then I learned that his confession had been faxed to Bulgaria. My heart was in my mouth. Surely the trial would be stopped? I was waiting for it to be dramatically called off at any moment, but instead it went on.

Our Joey was whispering to me that Sankey had signed his statement.

"Don't worry, we'll sue these bastards," he whispered. "He's signed it and they've received it over here."

Georgiev was always taking his cap off in court and rubbing the scar. If he honestly believed I'd done that to him, how could he sit there so close to me and look so calm? I noticed his dad was sat next to him. Whenever the TV cameras would come in he would nudge him and motion for him to rub his head. During his statement about his injuries, Georgiev said that because of his fractured skull, he couldn't even pick his baby up and he was extremely sensitive to the sunshine. On the last day, I glanced outside during a break and there he was; standing in the heat of the midday sun, holding his baby with one arm. His cap was nowhere to be seen. I started to get angrier – this was a stitch-up from every angle.

How could he do this? He was entitled to justice for what happened to him but why let the wrong person get framed? Still, I was more relaxed at the news about Sankey. I allowed myself to believe that it didn't matter what they said from then on. The trial had started on a Thursday and it was Friday afternoon. The court adjourned and they were set to start again for the final day on the Monday. Feeling buoyant, I went back to my cell and tried to explain the news about Sankey's confession to my cellmates.

One of them looked concerned and said that it may not matter because it wasn't made over here and Sankey wasn't in court. I went from elation back to despair. Suddenly the doubts were back in force and any positivity I felt vanished.

Luckily, my mates who'd managed to get over as witnesses were allowed to visit me that weekend. That picked my spirits up and I also saw my uncles and they said our Government would sort it all out now.

"They're not going to stand by and let an innocent lad get convicted, Mike," one of them said. "Especially now Sankey has thrown his hand in and made his confession."

I began to hope again. I hoped that the court session on Monday morning wouldn't even go ahead because of the confession, but sure enough it did. I'll never forget my dad's words to me over the phone that morning.

"Whatever they say to you, or whatever sentence they might give you, just take it on the chin and say you never did it."

There was something different about the journey to court. For a start, they put me in a white van which didn't smell quite so bad.

At the court, me and Wilson were sat there waiting to go in and I turned to him.

"Imagine if I got 15 years," I said. It was a joke at the time and I don't know what made it pop into my head.

"They wouldn't get away with it," said Wilson laughing. "They can't give you or me 15 years. Especially not me for a spliff."

This time there was more press than ever waiting for us. We had to push our way through as they jostled to take our picture and shout out questions. Half of the courtroom was cordoned off and the press were allowed to gather around, packed in tight.

Everyone was standing up and the judge came in and they all sat down except for us. Wilson was at my left, then a translator and then my lawyer. Wilson was to be first up. After speaking to him for about five minutes, the judge finished and made a hand motion. Wilson's lawyer turned to him, half-smiling.

"I've got a suspended sentence," said Wilson. He was grinning and looked at his lawyer.

"Yes, you're going home," said the lawyer as he folded papers. Everything seemed to go into slow motion and as I turned back to face the judge I heard: "15 years."

Suddenly it took me back to that bail hearing. Were they just discussing maximum sentences again? Then I heard "15 years" again and a noise throughout the court room, which to this day still makes me sick. It's like the sharp inhalation of breath, like the wince people make when someone gets hit or hurts themselves. I saw my lawyer bend over and scribble '15 years' on a piece of paper in front of him. Next to it he wrote: '200,000 lev.'

I desperately turned away from the judge looking for my uncle.

"What's going on?" I asked. "What's she on about?"

"Don't worry," said Joey. "It's getting dealt with."

But I was worried. In fact, I was so tightly wound I felt like I could burst. As I was led away from the bench, my head was completely gone. This one reporter shoved a microphone in front of my face.

"Is 15 years enough?" he asked.

I couldn't believe he'd just said it.

That's when I just flipped. I let rip.

"You are joking? Fuck off you cheeky bastard," I said, raging. My face was bright red and tears were streaming from my eyes. Two guards grabbed me and pulled me away. Out of the corner of my eye, I could still see Joey.

"Don't worry... the confession," he was saying.

I was surrounded by guards marching me out. I could see Wilson off to my left. He looked white but pleased to be going home.

"There'll be uproar over this back home," said Wilson. "Don't forget he's thrown his hand in."

"How have I just got 15 years?" I said. "How are they getting away with this?"

A big fat guard with white hair had hold of my collar and as he walked behind me he started kicking the back of my legs. They were short, vicious kicks into my calves. I was handcuffed and there was nothing I could do about it. I'll never forget his menacing red face. I've got nothing to lose now, I thought. I started going off at him.

"Fuck off you shitbag," I screamed. "Kicking someone in handcuffs."

I carried on screaming at him. They'd just ruined my life.

I'd been in shock until the journalist asked if 15 years was enough and that had opened the floodgates to anger. I caught sight of Andy Bonner, a TV news journalist from Liverpool.

"What have you got to say to the people back home?" he asked.

"Thanks for coming out here," I said to him. "Tell them that this is a sick joke and I'm not going to let it beat me."

TEARS OF MICHAEL SHIELDS' MOTHER AS HER INNOCENT SON IS JAILED FOR 15 YEARS IN BULGARIA FOR A CRIME HE DID NOT COMMIT
By Greg O'Keeffe

INNOCENT Michael Shields collapsed in a Bulgarian court today as he was found guilty of attempted murder.

Moments later he was given a 15-year sentence – five years more than the prosecution asked for.

Incredibly, the judge ruled he slammed a paving slab onto the head of a Bulgarian waiter, even though another Liverpool man has formally confessed.

Real attacker Graham Sankey, from Anfield, confessed to ensure Michael was set free.

"This has destroyed us," Michael's aunt Lin Graney told the Echo. Speaking after the verdict Shields's uncle, Joey Graney described the whole process as a "disgrace" and a "joke".

He added: "It's been a joke from start to end. None of the normal investigative measures you would expect to be carried out in a case as severe as this have been followed."

– Liverpool Echo, July 26, 2005

I HAVE NEVER SEEN SUCH A SWIFT INVESTIGATION AND TRIAL

Lawyer Oleg Antanasov said: "My client is innocent, but even if he had been guilty, this sentence is greatly exaggerated. Just last week this court sentenced a Bulgarian man who killed and chopped up his girlfriend to just 13 years in prison. And never before have I heard the court award more than 100,000 leva (£35,000) in damages. In 15 years of practising law I have never seen such a swift investigation and trial. They must have set a new record by completing it in two months."

– Shields' Lawyer Oleg Antanasov,
Liverpool Echo, July 26, 2005

REAL CULPRIT'S 'HORROR' AS REDS FAN IS SENT TO JAIL

By Greg O'Keeffe

REDS fan Michael Shields was today jailed for 15 years after a Bulgarian court found him guilty of a crime he did not commit.

The 18-year-old was convicted of a charge of attempted murder even though another man confessed to the crime.

The court in Varna refused to accept Graham Sankey's statement that he slammed a paving stone onto waiter Martin Georgiev's head at the resort of Golden Sands in May.

Today, Foreign Secretary Jack Straw was ordering officials and diplomats to "make representations" both to the Sofia legal establishment and to Bulgaria's ambassador to London, Lachezar Matev.

At Michael's home in Wavertree his devastated family said the "whole concept of justice had been ignored".

Graham Sankey's solicitor, David Kirwan, told the Echo his client was horrified by the verdict.

"Graham believed that the case against Michael would either be thrown out or adjourned after he came forward to make his confession," he said.

"But, to his total despair, the judge decided to continue trying Michael.

"Our focus at this time should be on Michael Shields, not Graham Sankey, and it is time for the British Government to intervene to make the Bulgarians see sense.

"The priority has to remain to get Michael Shields released from jail. Britons have a right to expect a fair trial if arrested abroad but Michael Shields is clearly getting nothing of the sort. It also causes me grave concern as to whether Graham Sankey would be treated fairly should he ever have to stand trial in a Bulgarian court."

Michael was also given a £71,000 compensation bill for the victim.

Fellow Liverpool fan Anthony Wilson, 19, was convicted of possession of marijuana and hooliganism. He was given a two-year suspended sentence and will now be allowed to fly home.

The Foreign Office wants assurances that a confession by Anfield electrician Graham Sankey is taken into account and say the question of bail for Michael pending further inquiries must be "thoroughly investigated."

The Echo understands that Mr Matev has already agreed to forward Sankey's crucial statement, provided it is signed and witnessed.

Sankey admitted that he, not Michael, was responsible for the attack, on their way home from Liverpool's Champions League victory in Istanbul, which led to the charge of attempted murder.

Fighting back tears, Michael's aunt, Lin Graney, said: "It's an absolute disgrace. How on earth can they come to this verdict when they know full well that there is someone in Liverpool who has confessed to it?

"It makes no sense and we just feel like the whole concept of justice has been ignored.

"They have used an innocent boy as a scapegoat because

they've arrested the wrong person for the crime in the first place.

"We had prepared ourselves for the worst because their justice system is a shambles but it's still so hard to take. Everyone at Michael's house today is devastated, we're all in pieces."

– Liverpool Echo, July 26, 2005

8. Guilty

By the time I returned to my pad, the news of my sentence had spread around the jail. As I walked along a corridor, I saw one of the guards tell another. I heard "15 years" and saw him wince. Even they couldn't believe it.

Ivan was waiting for me in the pad. He smiled and offered his hand in sympathy.

"My head was shot," I told him. Then a tear rolled down my cheek. "15 years," I said, and kept repeating it. "What sort of country is this?"

Ivan grabbed hold of my shoulders.

"Never cry," he said. "In prison, never cry. Never do that."

I understood what he was saying. To show emotion in prison is to show weakness. It was the last time I ever showed emotion over there. Straight away I snapped out of it and my head seemed to come together.

A guard came in a few minutes later and said I was getting a longer visit. An hour and a half. It was a strange visit, me and my uncles were laughing our heads off. I think that's all we could do to deal with what had happened. We weren't going to sit there and cry.

If you walked past the visiting room you wouldn't have thought that the lad inside had just been sentenced to 15 years in another country, miles away from home. Inside though, I still had the butterflies in my stomach. I was still barely eating. Every time the TV was switched on, it was in my face again. But gradually my mind started to become at rest. At least it was settled now. I started to feel calmer than I had been even before the trial.

I was allowed to make a phone call home and spoke to my mum. I kept getting told that everything was being sorted, that the whole thing was out of the court's hands now and it was a matter of our Government stepping in. It was only a matter of time. *When* it would be sorted out... not *if*.

CARRA CALLS ON BLAIR TO INTERVENE
By Tony Barrett

LIVERPOOL footballer Jamie Carragher today called on Tony Blair to intervene to win a reprieve for Michael Shields.

Speaking exclusively to the Echo, he said the Bulgarian court's decision to jail the 18-year-old Reds fan was such a grave injustice that the Prime Minister should get involved.

He said: "I don't know how the justice system works in Bulgaria, but hopefully something can be done.

"I think someone high up in the Government, possibly even Tony Blair himself, should step in and fight Michael's corner."

Carragher revealed that the team was thinking about Shields in the build-up to last night's Champions League clash with FC Kaunas.

"We got a phone call with the news yesterday but we've been aware of what's been going on throughout the whole trial," he said. "There was a banner about Michael at the TNS game in the last round and what's happened with the verdict was on our minds last night."

The match last night saw the defender score his first goal for six years – and he dedicated it to Michael.

He said: "If I'd known I was going to score, I would've worn a T-shirt under my shirt with Michael's name on it.

"I want to dedicate my goal to Michael Shields and all his

family. When we got the news that not only had he been found not guilty of a crime he didn't commit, but he'd also been sentenced to 15 years, our hearts sank.

"For myself, Steven (Gerrard) and the other local lads in the team, it really hit us. He's one of us, a young lad who went to a game to watch Liverpool and ended up being thrown in prison in a foreign country.

"He must be absolutely distraught at what's happened just as everyone in Liverpool is. He should've been here in Lithuania cheering us on but instead he's locked up. Me and Stevie are heartbroken for the lad because obviously it's an injustice."

He said that as Graham Sankey had admitted attacking Martin Georgiev the British Government had to intervene to secure Michael's freedom. "There is a lad in Liverpool who has owned up to the crime and admitted it was him."

– Liverpool Echo, July 27, 2005

We had two weeks to lodge an appeal against the sentence and that became my next goal. My legal team were going to use every bit of that time to gather more evidence and get more witness statements sent over from back home.

I was warned by my lawyers that this appeal was more of a formality, though, and not necessarily the one to get me out. Even then I was thinking: "OK, let's appeal against the sentence by all means, but I'll be out soon anyway." Then there was a breakthrough when I heard that Sankey had now taken the extra step of signing his confession.

SANKEY: I'LL SIGN CONFESSION
Exclusive by GREG O'KEEFFE

THE man behind the attack in the Michael Shields case today sensationally signed his confession, paving the way for Michael to be freed. Anfield electrician Graham Sankey, 20, agreed to sign the papers admitting it was he and not Michael who smashed a paving slab over the head of a 25-year-old Bulgarian bartender.

The breakthrough means innocent Michael, who was sentenced to 15 years for the attack on Tuesday, could now be free in months.

Sankey, currently in hiding with his family after receiving death threats, agreed to sign as it emerged that home secretary Jack Straw was to meet Michael's family at their Wavertree home. He had previously said he was prepared to stand trial for the attack only in a British court. But today's shock move means Bulgarian government officals can start the process of extraditing him.

— Liverpool Echo, July 28, 2005

I, GRAHAM SANKEY, WISH TO MAKE THE FOLLOWING CONFESSION:

On Sunday, May 29, 2005, I was in the Bulgarian resort of Golden Sands near to the Port of Varna at about 5am.

I unfortunately had far too much to drink; I had been drinking lager for the better part of the day.

In the evening I estimate that I drank nearly a full bottle of vodka and I was very, very drunk.

I left the PR Club and I was making my way to my hotel. I remember seeing a disturbance and a fight was taking place involving a large number of people, some of whom were wearing red shirts.

I could see bottles being thrown and as I drew closer a bottle smashed on the wall behind my head.

As I turned to see where the bottle had come from, I saw three men running at me with bottles and bricks in their hands. I panicked and stupidly picked up a brick and threw it in the direction of the men running towards me.

I saw the brick hit one of them. I panicked and I turned and ran away and returned to the hotel. I did not know at that time that Mr Martin Georgiev had been injured.

I was arrested (with others) by the Bulgarian police. The following day I was questioned by an investigator. I was utterly terrified and denied any involvement in the incident. I still did not know about the injuries to Mr Georgiev.

I was then released and I discovered that Mr Georgiev had been seriously injured. I then returned to Liverpool. I accept that I must have caused the serious injury to Mr Georgiev.

My conscience has been tormenting me ever since. I read in the papers about Michael Shields' trial, and I felt that I could not let an innocent man take the blame for what I had done.

So I instructed my solicitor, Mr David Kirwan, to make public my acceptance of responsibility and my willingness to accept fully the consequences of my actions. I expected that the Bulgarian court would accept my admission and free Mr Shields.

I was horrified that the court has refused to do this, so I am making this signed confession in the hope that an innocent man will no longer have to take responsibility for what I admit I did.

Finally, I want to say that I bitterly regret what I did to Mr Georgiev. I wholeheartedly apologise to him, his family and the Bulgarian authorities. I am only 20 years old, and am appalled that I have ruined Mr Georgiev's life and that Michael Shields, an innocent man, has received blame for what I did.

I just wish that I had my time over again.

Dated this 28th day of July 2005, signed Graham Sankey.

– The signed confession of Graham Sankey

While they were sifting through the mess of the trial, I found out something else which gutted me. The British witnesses who my defence wanted to call to come and give evidence for me only got their summons papers from the Bulgarian court office after I'd been tried and convicted. They never had a chance of getting over in time.

I was convicted and sentenced to 15 years while those subpoenas were still in the post. Everything worked so slowly over there. Or it did when it came to my case.

BULGARIAN LEGAL SYSTEM HAS LOST PEOPLE'S TRUST, SAYS TOP WRITER
By Greg O'Keeffe

JOURNALISTS in Bulgaria have reacted with shock at the rushed trial and 15-year sentence dished out to Michael Shields.

But only one Rupert Murdoch-owned national TV news station and a handful of English-language newspapers reported the amazing confession of Graham Sankey.

Other papers and media have portrayed Michael as a football hooligan, who got what he deserved.

Christina Dimitrova, news editor of national weekly Sofia Echo, wrote: "The sentence of Michael Shields to 15 years sent shockwaves throughout the Liverpool community.

"Whether Shields is guilty or not, we shall not discuss. That has been decided by the court.

"What is somewhat disturbing is that the court's decision has been contested by many who claim Shields is innocent, even more so after Graham Sankey admitted to committing the crime.

"What is even more disturbing is the fact that the court chose to ignore Sankey's confession."

She said Bulgaria was harshly criticised for its judiciary system and its "inability or unwillingness" to reform it.

"Many well-known members of organised crime syndicates walk the streets of the country as free men, in spite of having received several convictions.

"On many occasions the courts have handed down not guilty verdicts to people who have committed far more serious crimes.

> *"Such cases have brought considerable doubt for any court decision in this country and it is not surprising to hear the accusations of the Shields family, calling the trial a "circus" and a "miscarriage of justice."*
>
> *"It is rather hard to respect a decision handed down by a judiciary system which has long since lost the trust of the community."*
>
> *– Liverpool Echo, July 30, 2005*

As if that wasn't bad enough, I realised I had been wasting my time hoping that Sankey's confession would stop the trial. The judge had actually said he was not important as a witness and his confession meant nothing because it wasn't signed in Bulgaria.

How could they say that the confession of the lad who did it was unimportant to the case? We had been trying to say that the case needed to be delayed for Sankey to come over because he'd confessed, but they weren't interested in delaying it in time.

They kept referring to the original statement he'd given to police in Bulgaria when he was arrested and then allowed to go. That was when he'd denied having anything to do with it, which he was obviously going to do. How could they think that was plausible now when he'd since admitted it? He had gone to a lawyer and confessed. He'd now signed it. What statement were they going to believe in hindsight? My lawyer was saying it was vital we got Sankey over as soon as we could. "We can only ask him, though," I said. "We can't force him to come over here."

That sentence of 15 years lay heavy on my mind. It only really sunk in when I was doing an interview by phone with the BBC and the reporter asked me: "How do you feel possibly being here until you are 30?"

"I don't think that'll happen," I said. But deep down I wasn't so sure. I was hearing conflicting things from the other inmates'

AFTER THE TRIAL, I WENT OFF THE RAILS
– I WAS AT ROCK BOTTOM
By Michael Shields Senior

While I was over there waiting for the trial, Michael's friends also flew over to give their statements to the police. I felt sorry for them and I'll never forget John Unsworth's poor face after he'd come out from the police station.

"If you tell us any lies, you're not leaving this place," one of the detectives had told him. "We've got your passports."

They had come over to help their friend and tell the truth but they were traumatised. They had done nothing wrong either and just wanted to say they'd seen Michael in bed and that he'd had nothing to do with it.

During the trial, the prosecutor asked if I'd paid the lads to come over and give evidence – like I was rolling in money. It was degrading the way they were portraying us. Like we were gangsters who were trying to pervert the course of justice.

One of my biggest regrets was when I had to come home before the end of Michael's trial.

My 30-day visa had expired and I had to leave the country in order to be able to come back.

I sat through the first two days of the trial and then when it adjourned on the Friday, I flew home that evening and planned to fly back on the Sunday. But just when I needed one desperately, there were no flights back to Varna on the Sunday night. My heart was breaking. I needed to be by Michael's side for the verdict. It was due to arrive on the Monday.

Instead, I was sat at home with Maria when the phone call with the news came. Our world fell apart.

Then, within fifteen minutes, they came back with the sentence of 15 years and the massive fine. I was torturing myself. I should have just stayed over the expiry date of my visa, but that would have meant I couldn't go back for another six months. Thank God his uncle Joey was there for him, and at least I was there for Maria and the girls.

For a time after the trial, I went off the rails. I was at rock bottom. *I wasn't thinking enough about Maria or Michael or the girls, I was thinking about myself and my pain. I was struggling with getting out of bed in the morning knowing my son was locked up for something he didn't do.*

I started to drink heavier than usual to drown my sorrows. I wasn't drinking scotch, but I was having five or six cans of lager every night to try and help me sleep. I wouldn't go to the doctor and ask for sleeping tablets or anything like that.

I felt like I was fighting a corrupt state on my own and begging my Government to help and getting nowhere. My answer was to drink, and I hold my hands up and say now it was the wrong thing to do. It was my way of coping.

I eventually cut down on the drinking and realised I had to be there for my wife and son.

But nobody else knew how I felt.

I've blamed myself a lot. I still tell myself that it was me supporting football which is basically to blame for where Michael is. He was wrongly accused of something so serious – not stealing an apple from a shop, but trying to kill someone. I brought my son into the world not to hurt anyone. To be a good lad, which he has been.

I would like to see what other fathers would have done differently from me. I was laying in bed one night listening to the Pete Price radio phone-in show and somebody was asking how I could be in Liverpool while my 15-year-old son was still in jail in Bulgaria.

That hurt me badly so I phoned up and put the idiot straight. My son was 18, and I was back in Liverpool trying to get the support we needed to get his campaign up and running.

"He was an 18-year-old lad who went on holiday with his mates," I told Pete.

"I wonder if the last caller has teenagers? I wonder if they have ever let them go on holiday."

Generally, though, the city of Liverpool has been amazing. We come from a great city and they have stood behind us. No other city would have given us the kind of support that we have had.

Me and Maria have actually been sent on a trip to Lourdes – all paid for – by supporters of the campaign. It was magnificent. As I got on the plane, an elderly woman who seemed very poorly tapped me on the shoulder.

"How's your son, Mr Shields?" she asked in a Liverpool accent. "We're thinking of him." It was humbling.

Mass was said for Michael a few times when we were over in Lourdes. I'm a Roman Catholic and I did question my faith after it happened, but being in Lourdes made me feel a lot stronger.

It also put into perspective what happened to him, when I saw sick babies being pushed around Lourdes.

I said to Maria afterwards: "I can't have hatred in me – even for the people who did it. They've got to live with that."

At the same time, what saddens me is that the people who actually were responsible for the attack on Martin Georgiev are also from Liverpool and it gives the city a bad name.

The scale of what has happened still surprises me. Last year me and Maria went on a break to Benidorm for a few days and I got talking to a Chelsea fan from London at the bar.

We started to talk about football and had a bit of friendly banter. Then he brought Michael up.

"Is that young lad out of prison yet?" he asked.

"You know, the Liverpool fan – one of your lot.

"Has he been released yet? The Government should have done more for him." He didn't have a clue who we were.

"How are his mother and father?" he asked. "They getting more involved?"

"What's the real word on the streets in Liverpool about what happened?" he asked. "We only read about it in the papers. Do you think there's a chance the lad did it?

"No," I replied. "My son didn't." He nearly choked on his pint. "My son wouldn't hurt a fly," I said.

"I'm sorry mate," said the Chelsea fan. "I didn't mean anything by that."

We carried on talking and stayed on friendly terms for the rest of the break.

It wasn't long before my hopes were dashed over Sankey's signed confession. Prosecutors in Bulgaria said there was insufficient evidence to prompt an investigation.

Sankey had refused to travel to Bulgaria to answer questions. After he had signed his confession I thought he was going to come over and face up to it. It got my hopes up and I thought I might be home within a few weeks but now I knew that wasn't happening.

One night I was watching some highlights of European football on the little TV when part of a Liverpool game came on.

"You won't be watching them for a while," said one of the other prisoners casually.

He didn't mean it in a particularly nasty way but it did strike a chord. That feeling of being isolated and away from my old life got even stronger when the next Premier League season started. I knew my seat at Anfield would be empty.

I remember the first game of the season against West Ham because I was still keeping up with it. We'd just signed Peter Crouch and Daniel Agger. Agger scored and it looked like a really good game.

'I'd love to have been there watching that,' I thought. Still, I consoled myself with the thought that I'd be back watching it soon.

9. Sinking Deeper

The days rolled by, partly in a haze, and a fortnight passed. I was back in court for the appeal and there was my dad and sister. I waved to Melissa and laughed. It was probably nerves again, but I was ready for more comedy from the Bulgarian courts. My dad looked stressed, though, and whispered at me not to laugh or smile.

"Let them do what they want. I'm not bothered about them," I said to my dad.

While everyone else was standing respectfully in court, I just shoved my hands in my pockets and put my head down. How could I respect this circus of a court? Perhaps the judge sensed how I felt. She must have noticed my body language.

Dad must have taken what the psychiatrist said about me showing no remorse as a sign I should act sorry. Why should I, though? Why should I play that game of pretending to be sad for something I didn't do?

I scanned the court for Georgiev. No sign. He'd got his result in terms of the 200,000 Lev fine I'd been hit with and the compensation he'd receive out of that.

I wasn't even in court for an hour and it was over. They'd considered our initial appeal and would let us know. It's a good job I'd been warned not to get my hopes up for this one, because it would've been a major anti-climax.

Before we left the court, the judge asked if I had anything to say.

"We all know what happened. We all know this is a big charade," I said. "I'm only asking you – not telling you – to do the right thing."

Then the judge left and all the cameras started flashing again. I looked at my sister and started laughing at the ridiculousness of it. The nerves were making me act daft again. I could imagine my dad thinking: 'We're here trying to convince everyone he's innocent and here he is laughing in court.'

"Look sad," he was whispering to me. "Look sad."

Everyone was saying this is a serious situation and obviously it was. More serious than anything in my life had ever been.

But it was a mockery of justice.

I was thinking: 'Maybe some of these prosecutors and judges actually didn't really know what happened. If they did – how could they possibly stand here and call me a thug or an animal?' It was like something from a film.

News finally came that the initial appeal had failed. The local appeal court upheld my sentence but reduced the fine.

That also meant the compensation which Georgiev was going to get was cut to about £70,000. It was still a massive amount of money, enough to make him very rich over there.

It was also enough to make him the biggest target in Varna, especially when it was splashed all over the newspapers. It's a bandit country. Every gangster in Varna was probably rubbing their hands together getting ready to tax him.

The courts should have kept his payout quiet. My sympathy for him had diminished after all that had happened, but he had still suffered horrible injuries after the attack.

It was especially disappointing that the appeal had failed because new evidence had come to light around this time from a new witness who had come forward.

THE SWORN AND SIGNED EVIDENCE
OF WITNESS 'A' – IAN (Abridged)

We went out from the hotel to the Big Ben's fish and chip shop in Golden Sands. My girlfriend did not like any of the local food unfortunately, but did like the fish and chip shop. We were actually served by Martin Georgiev (the man who was attacked) at the chip shop where we had bought food several times earlier that week.

He was always great with us whenever we went in there. My girlfriend has a picture of us with him earlier on the same night the incident took place. I would say that Martin was a good fellow which is why I have a photograph of him with his arm around my girlfriend in the chip shop as a memory of the happy time we spent in the resort.

After we had our fish and chips dinner, we visited a couple of bars. I do not drink heavily and neither does my girlfriend. We both had a couple of bottles of Heineken imported beer to drink. My mother and father were with us as well. The third bar that we visited was on a corner of the street at the end of the same street in which our hotel was... by now it must have been 5.30am.

I could see a lot of the football fans in the bar because of the red colours and shirts that we had all agreed to wear. All of the fans were singing Liverpool songs. We were all joining in singing – it was, again, an absolutely brilliant night out. There was no trouble at all in the bar before the incident occurred.

I was standing outside the bar down the road from the hotel... Whilst I was at the bar, I noticed two young men; one with a white T-shirt and the other with a beige and blue striped T-shirt running down the road past the bar from the direction of the fish and chip shop. I could tell they were English and actually recognised them from the Kristal Hotel in connection with the incident when the money had been stolen. I did not know their names at that time...

One of them had a large bottle of beer in his hand and was emptying the contents of the bottle into the street. I immediately thought that this lad was intending to use the bottle as a weapon because I could see no other reason for emptying the beer on the floor...The lad with the bottle I would describe as quite small, no more than 5ft 6 to 5ft 7 inches tall. The other lad who did not have hold of any bottle was about the same height but had dark hair. He was the lad with the white T-shirt on. I saw the lad with the white T-shirt go behind a big waste container on wheels which was near to the electricity substation not far from the bar itself.

When he came back out from behind this large bin I saw that he had hold of something. I have been asked to remember very carefully what it was that I saw. What I saw was too large for a brick and too flat for a brick, and it looked to me to be a sandstone colour, and more of a rock than a brick. It must have been heavy because this lad in the white T-shirt was holding it close to his body with both hands as if it were heavy to hold. I saw these two lads turn and walk back towards Big Ben's fish and chip shop.

By now I was interested in what was going to happen, so I left the bar and crossed over the street in which the bar is situated to the opposite side... At the same time, I saw two young men running up the centre of the road in the direction of the bar being chased by 3 or 4 lads whom I recognised as part of this gang from the Sands hotel. These two lads ran into Big Ben's.

One of the lads who was chasing the lads up the street threw a bottle which smashed in the centre of the road outside the fish and chip shop as the lads ran inside, I think I saw the taxi driver who must have seen the bottle thrown and smashing in the street jump quickly into his taxi and drive off.

I saw one of the two lads who had been chased come to the doorway of the fish and chip shop, stop, and hold his hands above his head and I heard him shout, "Stop. We don't want any trouble." At this point I saw Martin come out and he told them to go away and leave, gesturing with his hand in a non-threatening manner to move on.

At this time I was gradually moving closer to the chip shop. One of the lads who had run past the shop turned around and seemed to see Martin who had come out of the chip shop. He started bouncing around on the balls of his feet like a boxer and made his way back towards Martin.

He then came face to face with Martin and I saw him strike a sudden blow with his right arm landing a blow to Martin's face. Martin must have been immediately knocked unconscious by this single blow because he fell forward face down in the road and not backwards. Martin did not move after he hit the floor and remained motionless face down.

I saw another youth run up and kick him whilst he lay on the ground. At this time the lad in the white T-shirt, who I have previously described, ran across the street from the opposite side around another parked taxi. I then saw him hit Martin on the head with this piece of stone that I have described. He did not raise the stone above his head, he was holding it about head height and brought it down sharply with force on Martin's head whilst Martin still lay unconscious in the road. I am still very upset and emotional when I think about what I saw... The whole incident I would say took no more than a couple of seconds from start to finish.

I did not know what to do. I went back to the bar and said to Claire she would never believe what I had just seen happen. The next morning when we got up to leave the hotel, someone said that somebody had been arrested for the attack on Martin. I thought it must have been connected with the police officer and the hotel porter rushing outside to arrest Anthony Wilson (after the attack) which it may well have been. Not for one moment did I dream the police had arrested the wrong man otherwise I would have made it my business to go and speak to the police about it. My girlfriend and family returned to England later that same day. It was only when I saw a photograph of Michael Shields that I realised the police had arrested the wrong man. I was able to see that Michael was a big lad and had blond hair. The lad in the white T-shirt who had dropped the paving stone on Martin's head was short and dark.

I should say, the same day before we took our plane home we made it our business to go back to Big Ben's. I spoke to a young man in the fish and chip shop who, although Bulgarian, spoke near perfect English.

He told me not to worry because there had been at least 10 people inside the fish and chip shop at the time of the attack and they were all capable of making a good identification of Martin's attacker. I remember that this lad who spoke perfect English was talking about English football hooligans in the area in general and said that they had all seen a fat lad with black hair attack Martin. As that was exactly the description I would have given police, I left believing that the Bulgarian police would arrest the right lad.

Before the trial, I saw a photograph of Michael Shields in the newspapers and realised that the Bulgarian police had the wrong man. However, I thought that the witnesses inside the chip shop would say that Michael did not match the description of the person who had attacked Martin. That is the reason why I did not come forward at the time to tell police I was an eyewitness to the assault. After Michael's trial, I was very upset to learn he had been convicted, but then almost immediately I heard that a lad called Graham Sankey had come forward to admit it, so I thought everything would be alright.

As time has gone by and I have read the various newspaper reports and listened to the radio, I have realised that the Bulgarian authorities believe they have the right man.

That is why I have now decided to come forward and give this statement. I am a person of good character and have no previous convictions.

– November 7, 2005.

BLOW TO JAILED TEEN MICHAEL
Exclusive By Greg O'Keeffe

TEENAGER Michael Shields today failed in a bid to have his 15-year sentence for the attempted murder of a Bulgarian barman reduced.

Appeal court judges ruled the 19-year-old student must serve the full jail term given to him following his trial in July.

Only one of the three-man review panel argued that the sentence should be cut. Reds fan Michael, from Wavertree, was convicted despite another man confessing.

Anfield electrician Graham Sankey admitted attacking father-of-two Martin Georgiev with a rock but has refused to face justice in Bulgaria. Michael, who has always said he was asleep when the attack took place in May, was given 15 years and his legal team instantly launched an appeal.

But judges today refused to consider any new evidence at the first appeal stage and only reduced Michael's fine to £40,000.

Now he faces a final make-or-break appeal against conviction at the Bulgarian supreme court in the new year. It comes despite a crucial new witness who has come forward to reveal he saw Sankey hit Mr Georgiev with a rock.

The Bootle man, who knew neither Shields nor Sankey, has even agreed to give evidence in Varna's county court.

Michael's MP Louise Ellman said: "It is bitterly disappointing but not entirely surprising because the court refused to listen to any new evidence including the Graham Sankey confession and new witness statements.

"The campaign for justice for Michael and his family will continue and all legal channels will be followed."

Liverpool Labour party leader Joe Anderson, who has campaigned on Michael's behalf, now hopes the new evidence will be considered by the supreme court.

He said: "We are sending this statement to the police and the court offices. I am disappointed by today's news, but I'm not giving up hope.

"Today was solely about reducing the sentence based on the original evidence – which we always believed was flawed.

"This new statement makes the hair stand up on the back of your neck. It speaks of the violent rock-slamming assault being carried out by Graham Sankey and the witness can prove he was at the scene."

– Liverpool Echo, November 9, 2005

So it was another blow but I'd been prepared for it. It was something I'd better get used to.

By then we'd already set our sights on an appeal at the Bulgarian supreme court in Sofia.

CAMPAIGNERS TAKE SHIELDS FIGHT TO NO.10

FAMILY and friends of jailed teenager Michael Shields delivered an 80,000-name petition to Downing Street.

They were calling on the Government to lobby the Bulgarian authorities and make every effort to secure Michael's release from his 15-year sentence.

The Prime Minister was not available to meet the family, but they were assured by foreign office minister Douglas Alexander that the UK would provide the 19-year-old from Wavertree with full legal and consular support.

The delegation was taken to Downing Street by Riverside Labour MP Louise Ellman.

She said: "He told us he would continue to raise this matter with his counterpart in Bulgaria but he stressed he could not interfere in the Bulgarian judicial system.

"He believed the important thing now was to focus on the appeal."

– Liverpool Echo, December 1, 2005

The days in prison came and went, playing cards, reading more books than I'd ever imagined I could, learning more snippets of Bulgarian and grabbing exercise when I could. In the meantime, I was having the odd visit from my lawyer and we were preparing for Sofia. I managed to keep my spirits up by using the bits of Bulgarian I'd learned to play tricks on the guards.

When a guard came into the cell, we all had to stand up, but one day I stayed seated.

"Stand!" he shouted in English, looking irritated. Then again, this time less sure. "Stand."

I was pretending to look confused and I could tell he was wondering about his own English. Suddenly, he hit on a solution thinking he must have mixed his commands up.

"Sit!" he ordered. Instantly I stood up, keeping my face deadly serious, knowing how confused he'd be after inspection. Other times guards would walk past and I'd say something in Bulgarian and the guards would peer in, blaming the other lads inside and I'd be laughing my head off. After a year-and-a-half, I was almost fluent in Bulgarian, and when I later got back to the UK, I was more used to writing with the Cyrillic alphabet than the Western one. I learned most of it from watching the TV news. It didn't take me long to learn that: 'Петнадесет години' meant '15 years'. Whenever my face flashed up on the screen, they'd say that at some point. I hated seeing myself on the TV.

One day I received some news which really messed with my head. Sankey had retracted his confession.

Via his solicitor he had claimed that he hadn't attacked Georgiev after all and the attack he had confessed to was separate. To this day, there has never been any report of another Bulgarian being attacked that night.

There were no witnesses to that so-called separate attack. Equally, if there had been another Bulgarian victim in that resort, they would have come forward for their justice... their compensation. There can be no doubt about that. Once again my brain was tying itself in knots.

How do you retract a confession? Once you've said something, it's said. You couldn't walk into a police station covered in blood and tell them you've just killed your mate, only to change your mind half an hour later and say: "Nah, sorry. I retract it."

It didn't make any sense. We still needed to use that statement as best as we could, because as far as I was concerned, it still stood.

I was more bewildered than angry. In my mind I just rubbished the news. Surely there could simply be no such thing as a retracted confession?

I told myself that no matter what he says now he has still admitted it and it was still useful. Sankey had obviously been feeling the pressure and saw what had happened to me and thought: "I don't want to go over there and get 15 years."

SANKEY: I DIDN'T DO IT
By Greg O'Keeffe

GRAHAM Sankey today sensationally claimed he was NOT behind the attack for which Michael Shields is serving 15 years in a Bulgarian jail.

On the steps of Liverpool Magistrates' Court, just minutes after contesting a police bid for a football banning order, Sankey's solicitor read a statement in which the burly Anfield electrician retracted his confession.

As Sankey lurked inside the court, his legal team insisted that after careful examination, they were confident the attack he admitted to was different to the one in the Shields case.

Reading the statement, solicitor David Kirwan said: "The Sankey family and myself are at a loss to understand why Merseyside Police have chosen to bring these proceedings against my client.

"Graham Sankey has never been involved in a football-related incident in this country and the police application concerns an incident on foreign soil for which he has never been tried, let alone convicted.

"We believe strongly that there is no foundation whatsoever for this action and would call upon the police to reconsider their position.

"There are serious discrepancies between the evidence in the Bulgarian court in the Michael Shields case and the statement made by my client on July 28 last year.

"It is our belief that we may be talking about two entirely separate incidents."

He added: "There has been no contact from the Bulgarian authorities with my client."

– Liverpool Echo, March 9, 2006

10. Justice and Hope

The day we went to Sofia is still crystal clear in my mind. Sofia prison was massive. It just seemed to go on and on. It was right in the middle of the capital city and I would be there for a few days because my appeal was on the list for later that week. A new prison always means a whole new set of problems to sort out, new fears. It could mean a new person snarling in your face from day one. It's like all the things you've achieved in adapting to one place being ripped up and thrown in the air.

In Sofia there were 10 wings on each floor and it was really scary. The corridors were all narrow and winding. As they led me in I saw a sign which said "Danger Wing" on it. I was with a Bulgarian kid who had his appeal too and they led us into one of the danger wing doors. "Surely not," I was saying to myself.

Ivan had told me I'd probably get put in a special holding cell for foreign nationals while I was there, but here I was going on this danger wing.

I'd been looking forward to going in a foreign national cell and maybe even meeting someone who could speak some English.

The danger wings are for people with no parole. Lifers, who are in for the really bad stuff.

I didn't want to imagine that. As I was walking through, my head was all over the place and that's when I realised that the foreign national holding cell was in the danger wing. I wasn't going to have to go in with the lifers after all.

I had a little bag of stuff with me like a toothbrush and some soap and that was about it. This guard came over to me and kept asking if I had a SIM card. I told him I didn't, but I had loads of phone cards. Probably £100 worth off my dad. He just kept asking about SIM cards in broken English. As with most of the guards, I couldn't get what he meant and vice versa.

They brought me some food down while I waited; a boiled egg and a bag of oily fish. I hated that oily fish back in Varna and it was Sod's law I'd got it there, too. I'd be smelling nice for court. It might not have been for lifers, but the holding cell area was still horrible, it was more like a dungeon. Each cell had a grim metal door and there were five people inside mine and one bed.

It was mid-morning. Before they left me, one of the guards motioned to my trainers and made a gesture for me to take them off. I handed them to him and he pulled out the laces with a bored expression on his face. It was in case I decided to use them to hang myself. I glanced at the shoes of the other four lads in the cell, theirs were all gone, too.

At night, you'd hear even more screaming. The only good thing about Sofia was being able to look out over the lights of the city at night. It's the capital and it would be nice seeing how busy it was with all those people whizzing around getting on with normal lives.

Normality was miles away for me. It was going to stay that way for a long time, too.

I quickly befriended an Armenian lad who spoke a tiny bit of English and gave him some phone cards. It was a good way of getting lads onside.

It was the same with Ivan. When he trusted me he let me know he had a mobile, although he insisted I kept quiet about it. Again, I was able to give him the credit with phone cards.

It's only through getting to know people like Ivan that I learned how things were. How life in a Bulgarian jail worked.

That's what I've always done really. Just looked for a friendly face. Anywhere new I went, I'd look for a face that seemed less hard than the rest, even just a little bit. Someone who looked like they had a bit of decency about them.

SHIELDS TRANSFERRED TO LARGER PRISON
By Greg O'Keeffe

MICHAEL Shields is to be moved to a new prison in the Bulgarian capital before his make-or-break final appeal.

The 19-year-old, from Wavertree, will be transferred to a larger prison in Sofia ahead of a Supreme Court appeal against his 15-year sentence in January.

His legal team hope new evidence revealed by the Echo could lead to a retrial or the extradition of the man who has admitted to the attack Michael was accused of carrying out.

Michael has always insisted he did not slam a paving stone over barman Martin Georgiev's head in the Golden Sands resort in May.

He was convicted and sentenced despite Graham Sankey signing a confession and has spent the last eight months in Varna prison, on the Black Sea coast.

On Monday, the Echo revealed how a new witness has come forward with vital evidence.

His statement has been signed, approved by the British Government and sent to the Bulgarian courts.

Today, his family and campaign team welcomed the move as they continued to lobby the Government for support.

City Labour leader Joe Anderson said: "It means Michael will be near to where the next legal action is going to take place. We really hope that this new evidence could make the Bulgarian prosecutors consider a retrial or even just the straight extradition of Sankey."

Merseyside Euro MP Arlene McCarthy has already claimed

that breaches of the European Convention on Human Rights have occurred over the access Michael's legal team have had to potential evidence during his case.

And Michael's Riverside MP Louise Ellman won an adjournment to discuss Michael's legal fight in the House of Commons.

Mrs McCarthy this week made a formal complaint about the appeal procedure to European President Joseph Borrell.

— Liverpool Echo, December 8, 2005

Sofia Supreme Court was only the second court I'd ever been to in my life and I was flabbergasted by the size of it. Before I was finally led into court, I was given my shoelaces back and then taken in alongside seven other prisoners, all handcuffed together in a row. The court was full of marble arches and brass benches. Very grand – it took my breath away. Then I spied the press again and thought: 'Here we go again.' It had been a while since I'd seen the press.

The court had 10 rows of benches either side of a main walkway up to the bench. The cameras were snapping away as soon as I walked in and I felt a flash of temper. There was my mum standing there in the public area – the last thing I wanted was for her to see me like this, standing there handcuffed to other prisoners. I smiled at her and she was looking alright so that gave me a bit of reassurance.

The three judges seemed to be sat miles away from us and I also saw one of my uncles sat in the public area. As I stood there, I could feel my hand getting pulled to the right. The guy handcuffed to my right was trying to turn himself around and pulling me with him, he didn't want to be filmed by the TV cameras.

"Stop it," I said as he was pulling me. But I didn't blame him.

My dad had told me to stick to the truth again in Sofia, but I wondered what good it would do. Suddenly, amongst the media pack I spotted Andy Bonner again. As the hearing began, the guard unlocked the handcuffs and I quickly turned and shook Andy's hand.

"Thanks for coming," I said. The prisoner next to me wasn't happy as I moved to shake Andy's hand and he was dragged back into range of the cameras. It felt good that one of those TV crews was actually from my home city and would be supporting me instead of labelling me a hooligan.

One by one the prisoners along the row walked up to the front and had their cases heard. As each returned and my turn grew closer, the nerves set in. I couldn't see my lawyer anywhere and mouthed a question to my dad. "Where's Rick Astley?" but I couldn't hear his response. A moment later, a suited man I didn't recognise entered the court and sat behind me. He quickly whispered to me that his name was Georgi Gatev and he was my new lawyer. Any doubts I had disappeared when I was called up. I think he cost a lot of money but he seemed to be worth it.

Gatev got up to present my appeal and he was brilliant. He absolutely wasted the case against me. Going through every point meticulously and rubbishing all their claims, he seemed very convincing. The translator whispering in my ear had trouble keeping up with him he was that fast. I allowed optimism to overtake me. 'I'm going home here,' I thought. Anyone listening to this man can't fail to agree with him. He really was the business.

The prosecutor got up and even he was making sympathetic noises, saying he was aware of how young I was and how long the sentence was. 'That's all well and good,' I thought, 'but get on and talk about the case.' I wanted them to go over the case again. To accept it wasn't me. Instead, the prosecution were saying that no further evidence had come to light that suggested I was not the guilty man. I couldn't believe it. Was Sankey's confession really not worth the paper it was written on? What about the other witness? Then a private prosecutor, on behalf of Georgiev, got up and started talking in a shrill, squeaky little voice.

Once she'd said her bit, the appeal was finished and they told

Gatev they would notify us of their decision via letter. I felt fairly positive, after all, Gatev had been amazing in there.

The press descended again as we were led out and I had to bite my lip to stop from shouting that they'd get a shock when the appeal came back and cleared me. Then all I wanted to do was to get 'home' to Varna as quickly as possible. I'd had enough of Sofia; its jail and its gigantic, intimidating court. I still felt really positive with what I'd heard in court.

As we were getting ready to go, the guards were dishing out little bags with some food in for the long trip back. Inside mine was the usual; a boiled egg, two pieces of bread and oily fish. I wished it was the feta cheese and olives that we got in Varna prison and was tempted to ask for some of that but thought better of it.

'Don't speak to them,' I thought. 'They probably look down on people from Varna here.'

Outside the prison was a big blue coach which we were to be driven back in. It was caged and I was pushed in and had my ankles and wrists handcuffed to the man next to me. Just as the coach pulled away, I had that panicky feeling you get when you know you've left something behind and there's nothing you can do about it. I'd left a little crucifix which my sisters gave me behind in the cell. I was gutted because it'd been a lucky charm for me. Well, it'd been a charm anyway.

I was four prisoners away from the front of the coach and a few of the guards had guns. It was like something from the movie 'Con-Air' with Nicholas Cage. It was extremely uncomfortable and hot on the coach, and as the long journey wore on, I started to feel nauseous and cramped. Around about 12pm, we stopped at a prison in a place called Lovidge and we were allowed to get some fresh air. It was blazing hot outside and as we were led to a small yard, I was still handcuffed to the prisoner next to me. The fella I was joined to spoke English, which was a bonus. I asked him if he would mind walking over to the toilet area because I was desperate to splash some water in my face. As we shuffled towards the toilets, I saw little orange dots flashing in front of my eyes. The sun was pounding down and the orange dots gave way for flashing stars. My legs went weak.

The next thing I knew I woke up with a jolt as cold water was being poured over my head. A big Alsatian one of the guards had was next to me panting in the heat.

"What happened?" I managed to murmur. I felt groggy and like I'd just woken up from a deep sleep. Someone explained that I'd collapsed. Probably from heat exposure, exhaustion, or both. Maybe the appeal day had stressed me out and caused my body to flip on me. I really just wanted to get back to Varna and the environment I'd grown used to. I wanted to get something to eat that didn't make me retch, and phone my mum. The lad who was handcuffed to me had mud and white dust all over his jumper.

"What happened?" I asked him.

"As you fell, I fell with you," he said matter-of-factly.

Instead of putting us back on the 'Con-Air' coach, they decided to walk us into the centre of Lovidge. We were walking along in the heat like a chain-gang and it was like being herded along Church Street in Liverpool city centre on a Saturday afternoon. There were people everywhere and they were all staring and pointing. 'I really don't need this,' I thought as a child pulled his mum's sleeve and pointed.

After a thankfully short walk, we stopped and got put into a little van, where we sat waiting. Again. I was sick and tired of waiting all the time. A few shards of sun lit up the gloomy little van and the material of the seats was uncomfortably hot to touch. I felt like I was on my last legs and as if I might collapse at any time, but at least we were on the final stretch back to Varna. As we drove along, I continued to chat to the lad next to me. He was the opposite of me, in that he was from Sofia and had liked being in Sofia jail and now he was being moved to Varna. He was dreading it because he didn't know what to expect. As we got closer, he got more nervous.

"Don't worry," I said, trying to be reassuring. "It's brilliant in Varna. I'm happy to be going there."

The engine stopped and I got a warm sensation. We were back in Varna. The doors at the back of the van opened and there, grinning, was one of the Varna guards.

"What are you doing back here?" he asked. I laughed as he helped me out of the van and then hesitated, waiting for orders.

"What are you waiting for?" he asked good-naturedly. We had often joked about football in the past and I was on first name terms with him. "Go on. Go up to your cell. You know what to do."

Even that little bit of personal freedom, not being shoved and bossed about, was great. Being treated less like a prisoner, even if it was only a fraction. The instant I was in my cell and the door had shut I was on my craftily stashed mobile, phoning home for news.

Later that evening I found out that the lad who was nervous about coming to Varna had good reason. He'd been put on the wing below mine where they put the homosexuals and the sex offenders. It was because he was only staying for a few weeks and my wing was full. I caught up with him in the yard the next day and he said he was here on a drug-dealing charge. He was worried he could get up to 20 years. Again, I tried to reassure him, but after what had happened to me, it was anyone's guess what could happen.

We struck up a friendship and spoke when we could. I soon learned what happened to paedophiles in a Bulgarian prison. They did not get their own isolated wing like in British prisons, the system did them no favours.

My friend was one of many lads on non-sex offence charges mixed in with the paedophiles. He said there were two big guards who would go into a different child molester's cell every night and batter them. If they were sentenced to life with no parole, it was their best chance of surviving because only then did they get a small degree of protection in a separate wing. If they got life with chance of parole, they stayed on the mixed wing with the other offenders and the gypsies. Then, my friend said, they'd be lucky to survive the first year. They'd either get beaten to death, get stabbed or be driven to suicide. Either they lived with no hope of ever seeing the free world again, but at least a chance of living, or they almost certainly died. Simple as that.

It scared me because I immediately imagined someone who might be down there who was wrongly convicted. Someone sentenced on a misunderstanding like me who was going to die. I couldn't allow myself to think about it too much. The majority of people inside any prison will admit there's a reason they are locked up. It's only a few who will protest their innocence. Yes, lots of people object to their sentence, but not many could or would say: "It wasn't me."

It's never worth unloading your problems to other prisoners because everyone inside has problems. Some people have got little babies outside who they miss badly. Others have got sick wives or parents. They may have money problems or be fighting their own appeal. It's depressing to harp on about your situation all the time.

We'd been told in Sofia that we'd get the results of the appeal in 30 days, but 30 days passed without any response. Two people from the Foreign Office came to see me in that time, a man and a woman with London accents, and they promised to let me know as soon as they heard anything. A couple of days later, I got word they were downstairs to see me and, taking a deep breath, I went to meet them.

They were in an office and asked me to sit down.

"OK Michael," said the woman. "We've had the response from Sofia and while they haven't overturned your sentence, they have cut it from 15 years to 10. At the same time they have increased the fine you've got to pay."

It took a while for the news to sink in. They must have had some pull, the Foreign Office pair, because the lieutenant of the prison let me make a call to my parents there and then. They were in the hotel in Varna waiting for the news. They were both upset and crying a bit during the call but they said the wheels were in motion for me to be transferred to a British prison. I told my dad to take my mum home and relax. I knew I'd get nothing from the Bulgarians now.

SHIELDS FAMILY DEVASTATED: FIVE YEARS OFF SENTENCE – BUT NO RETRIAL
By Graham Davies

THE father of jailed football fan Michael Shields said last night he was "devastated" after a Bulgarian court denied the teenager a retrial.

Shields, 19, was serving 15 years in a Bulgarian jail for the attempted murder of a barman in the Black Sea resort of Golden Sands last May.

Shields appealed against his conviction to Bulgaria's Supreme Court last month.

He hoped the court would either overturn the conviction or at least grant him a retrial.

The court yesterday reduced his sentence from 15 to 10 years but refused to grant a retrial. It also re-imposed a fine of £71,000, which had been reduced to £42,000 at an earlier appeal.

It is now hoped the teenager will be transferred to a British jail to serve the rest of his sentence.

Shields's father, also called Michael, said the reduction in sentence was "no comfort whatsoever".

He said: "We are so angry and disappointed, we're devastated. I'm just baffled by the way this country works.

"We were hoping the court would overturn Michael's conviction, or give him a retrial so he could prove his innocence.

"Instead, they have just knocked five years off his sentence, which is no comfort to me whatsoever because my son is innocent.

"Not only that, but they have increased the fine back to its original level. I can't understand how they can reduce the sentence but increase the fine."

Mr Shields and his wife, Maria, had travelled to Bulgaria to be near their son when the appeal decision was made.

It was due to be made last week and the pair were about to fly home when news finally arrived. They now plan to stay for several more days to visit their son.

The family will also ask for Shields to be transferred to a British prison.

Mr Shields said: "We're quite hopeful we can get Michael moved to a British jail, because the Bulgarians said that when he was originally sentenced.

"He had to stay in Bulgaria while the appeal was ongoing but that is over now, so the plan is to get him back to England and then continue fighting to prove his innocence."

– Liverpool Daily Post, April 29, 2006

Ataturk: The atmosphere in the stadium was amazing, it was a sea of red

Trial: Waiting to hear my fate alongside Anthony and our interpreter

Devastated: I kept screaming my innocence as I was bundled out of court

Stunned: I couldn't believe I had just been sentenced to 15 years of hell

Tearful: My eyes just welled up as I faced the glare of the media

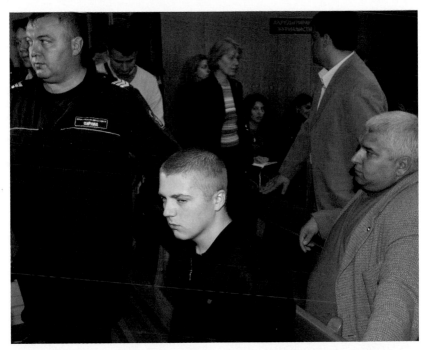

Appeal: Back in court, but attempts to get my sentence reduced failed

Hope: My Bulgarian lawyer Georgi Gatev talks to my parents about a retrial

Victim: Martin Georgiev with wife of key witness Ian – who said I was innocent

Scarred: Georgiev shows the courtroom the wounds he suffered in his attack

Confessor: Graham Sankey

Overjoyed: My mum holds up a copy of Sankey's signed confession

Visit: Mum and dad outside the prison in Varna a year on from the trial

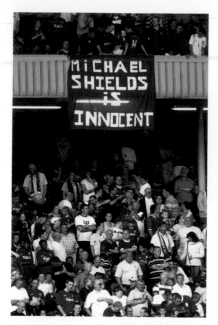

Solidarity: The moving messages at Anfield kept my spirits high

Support: Banners and posters around my hometown of Wavertree

Comforted: Mum and dad surrounded by messages of support back home

Bookworm: Reading helped detract from the boredom, if only for a short while

Harry Kewell limp off. The player who come on went on to play brilliant. 2-0 come and we could feel it slipping. I was dry so I went up to get some drinks and then heard another roar and in my head it was over.

Half-time come and everyone was deflated. The feeling was that we we're playing for pride now and all the fans starting singing Walk on and we're gonna Win 4-3. I said to Spud that if we score a goal in the first ten minutes anything could happen but deep down it was a dream. The players come out for the second half and it was a relief more than anything to see Hamann come on. The fans started to sing walk on again and that was it, 45 minutes to go and we begin the journey home. Nothing can ever prepare us for what happened next, as we are watching it I'm refusing to believe it could happen. 3-1 and it was more believe. 3-2 and we couldn't believe what we we're seeing. 3-3 and it was chaos. But the moment we knew we would win it was when Dudek made that sa Shevchenko, we knew fate.

Journal: An extract from the diary I kept while serving my sentence

Mail: Receiving letters from home gave me a lift but it was also tinged with sadness

11. Spirit of Liverpool

While I was in Bulgaria, I was aware that there was a lot being done back at home to help my cause. I'll always be grateful to everyone who backed the campaign to get me released. In a way, it doesn't surprise me. That's what Liverpool people are like – they look after their own. Councillor Joe Anderson was involved in my case right from the start. This is his story.

The office phone rang. It was one of my councillors explaining that a woman from Edge Hill wanted to talk to me about her son. He'd been locked up in Bulgaria and they were insisting the police had the wrong man. I had an hour or so free, so I went to speak to her. I'm a firm believer in grass-roots politics and elected members serving their community.

It's still crystal clear in my memory that first time I sat down with Maria. She told me about what had happened, about the type of lad Michael was, and how he was being accused of something he simply hadn't done.

Even though I hadn't met him, I began to get the feeling something wasn't right about his arrest and that feeling only got stronger. Maria was crying and I looked her in the eyes and said I'd do everything I could to help. I could never have imagined how big this case was to become over the next five years.

The first thing we did was organise a demonstration and phone the Liverpool Echo to get some publicity. I quickly outlined what had happened to the reporter. He said they were going to run a story about Michael in the next edition.

I was stunned at how many people showed up at the demo. It was a mixture of fans and their families who'd been over in Istanbul and friends of the Shields. The amount of support just confirmed to me my gut feeling that this lad was innocent.

We got someone to video the day and posted the tape over to Michael in the hope he could watch it, and see the instant support he had back home. That demo really spurred us on and I remember saying I would stay with it and not give up until we got him out. Again, I couldn't imagine it would become a full-time job involving 30 visits to see Michael in five different institutions, two countries and countless hours travelling.

After the demo, I wanted to go and see him and talk to him myself. I hadn't been apprehensive in pledging my total backing but I wanted the reassurance of at least meeting him face to face. I suppose there was an element of risk because I hadn't been there on that night, but my instincts told me he was innocent.

I approached my party members and told them I wanted to fly to Bulgaria. Straight away they were fantastic and supportive. The old Lord Mayor Jack Spriggs said the party would pay for it. No problem.

My flight went from Heathrow to Vienna and then into Varna. The first thing I did was to go and see Petr Kandilarov, who was an elected Mayor, Varna's version of Ken Livingstone. I was treated like Royalty at his office.

Straight away I apologised on behalf of the people of Liverpool for what had happened to Martin Georgiev, but said that on the basis of what I knew, they had got the wrong man. He was supportive and helped arrange the visit to the prison which was to be the next day.

That evening, I went down to the hotel bar for a pint on my own and reflected on my first impressions of the country. The sun was shining outside and I took a quiet walk to get my bearings. I was overwhelmed by the amount of beggars. A little girl ran over touching my leg and asking me to buy some tat from her. I gave her some money and she ran away but a few minutes later she was back over. It was a familiar pattern. Increasingly, I realised the majority of people there were 'on the take'. The taxi drivers would try and kid you over the fare, a shopkeeper would try and charge you more than the real price, everyone wanted money from you.

The next day, I went to see Michael and the cab driver on the way was trying to sell me things. I already knew the fare, but he wanted to charge me double that amount.

Rain was lashing down as I met the interpreter outside the Varna detention centre and walked into the courtyard. It was like a scene from the film 'Midnight Express'.

You could smell the stench of sewerage and urine and the building was crumbling. I walked into a courtyard and was led up a flight of stairs. In the background you could hear prisoners shouting to each other. It was like one of the old-fashioned jails from a film.

The guards led me to an office where Michael was waiting. His mum and dad had told him I was on the way, and we sat down and spoke for about an hour-and-a-half.

First we spoke about how he was being treated and how well he was. As a parent myself and a trained counsellor who has worked with young people for many years in my day job at a school, I knew this was a kid who wasn't capable of carrying out such a vicious attack on anyone.

I told him I'd do everything I could for him and how determined I was to help his family. I told him I believed him, and then I had to leave. I was quite moved when I had to walk away because you could see he was distressed. He was in a foreign country and knew things were being said about him in the Bulgarian press.

He was an 18-year-old lad, in some senses immature for his age, and the worry was that someone would do something to him after reading he was a so-called English thug... an 'animal' who was accused of dropping a brick on the head of a Bulgarian waiter.

I left with a heavy heart, wishing I could do more to help.

Later that day, I met with his legal team and shook hands with his first lawyer over there. He'd been recommended as a great legal mind by Petr Kandilarov, but he was hopeless. He didn't instil me with any confidence and I could tell he was bluffing it, even though his English wasn't perfect.

"Don't worry. It's all in hand," he said. "I know this system."

I just had to leave it hoping that things would get better. There was time for one last trip to the British embassy to check they were doing their part before I flew home.

From there it really began in earnest. Constantly ringing Bulgaria and setting up fundraising events at home. Arranging to get Louise Ellman on board and convincing her to lend her vital support. It was frustrating dealing with the cultural and linguistic divide with Bulgaria, but much worse knowing their judicial system and police were so terribly poor in how they conducted themselves.

When Michael was telling me about his arrest, I was more and more appalled. How could he be chained to a radiator in full view of witnesses? Driven back to the crime scene in front of more witnesses? Forced to wear a white T-shirt he didn't even own let alone have on in the ID parade? It beggared belief.

Michael's lawyer insisted he knew what the issues were and was dealing with them. I was very much in his hands, but in hindsight we would have done so many things differently.

There is an eye witness from Merseyside called Ian who saw the attack on Martin Georgiev. I only met Ian much later, after putting a council motion down from the town hall for any witnesses to come forward.

He got in touch with me some four months after it had happened, but it turned out he had already given a statement to Michael's first lawyer who had sat on it. He'd decided not to use it early on but to save it.

This was a statement from someone who didn't know the two lads involved in the attack but who had seen them causing trouble in his hotel earlier during his break in Bulgaria. He was able to say not only that Michael wasn't the attacker, but that he was not even there – and for some reason it wasn't used early.

When he spoke to me, I immediately got it notarised by a solicitor and sent straight over to Bulgaria, but valuable time had passed and it was only ready for the appeal. The appeal court turned around and said that because it hadn't been used in the trial, it couldn't be used in the appeal. It was outrageous.

Ian was a totally objective witness. He knew neither the real attackers or Michael, but just wanted the truth to come out. We lost the appeal. People questioned Ian then and said why didn't he come forward earlier, but he had done. What had really happened was astounding. Ian's girlfriend had actually befriended Martin Georgiev during the holiday, because they ate in Big Ben's fish and chip shop where he worked regularly. They even posed for a smiling picture together.

After seeing the attack, Ian was sickened. He went to the restaurant the next day to ask how Martin was and if the police needed anything. The staff there said it was OK. They'd seen the stocky man do it. Based on what they told him, he assumed they had identified the real attacker and flew home later that day confident justice would be done.

It was only when he read the Echo that he realised the wrong man had been arrested. But then Sankey confessed and he thought it was resolved once and for all. Of course, Sankey then retracted his confession and Ian came forward and gave his statement to the solicitor, who sat on it for the appeal.

He must have wondered what had happened and why his statement wasn't used, so he responded to my witness call from the town hall. If things had been done differently, Michael might not have done four years.

Sankey retracting his confession was a big smack in the face. I went to see his dad at his house in Anfield and could hear noises from upstairs where Graham was moving about.

I sat down with his dad for a chat.

"How do you know it was him?" his dad said. "Graham says it wasn't him."

"People have identified him," I replied. "There's an innocent

man in prison here. Graham's even admitted it and then changed his statement on his solicitor's advice." He told me he felt sorry for Michael Shields, but refused to budge.

I tried a different tack. If Graham was willing to admit he'd done it once and for all, I would offer him all the support I could and try and ensure he was treated fairly. We got nowhere. Blood is thicker than water, as they say, and he defended his son.

I phoned him a few months later asking if Graham would at least come out and say Michael Shields wasn't there.

"I'll talk to him," was all he said. I never heard from him again.

After Michael's sentencing, the courts imposed a massive fine of around £97,000 – one of the highest they'd ever imposed on a foreigner. It was like they were saying: 'We won't have football hooligans coming over here and doing this', and they were sending out a message. The sheer size of the fine shocked many people, aside from the sentence.

I remember losing the final appeal in Sofia, after we'd put forward a strong dossier of new evidence including the Bulgarian concierge who described seeing Michael go up to bed hours before the attack. He described the brace on his teeth and the three-quarter-length shorts he was wearing.

They even dismissed the evidence of the lads who saw Michael asleep in his bed because they were his friends. There was a Finnish girl who was half-asleep in the room who heard Michael come in and go to bed, too.

It seemed no matter what we did or said, we simply weren't going to get anywhere with the Bulgarians.

The biggest challenge was to get him home and that meant raising £97,000, but at the same time we needed to keep paying for the visits of Michael's mum and dad, which were costing a couple of thousand pounds a time. Those visits were keeping him going. The phenomenal support we had from the people of the city was sustaining those visits. Michael Snr and Maria Shields had to give up their jobs so they had no income. The strain of going over there constantly was hurting them, too.

After the appeal failed, I said to Maria again: "Don't worry, I'll raise that money. We'll get him home." But I thought to myself: 'What are you saying?' We had three months to raise £97,000 and somehow we did it.

It was a tremendous effort. We had a campaign office with a phone and a computer near the Shields' home in Towerlands Street and I set about ringing people and asking them for money, in some cases begging them.

A businessman from Wirral, Gerry White, couldn't do enough for us. He told me to buy a brand new car and raffle it.

"I'll pay for it," he said. "Just get a car and whatever you make from the raffle is for the campaign."

We went and bought one that day and took it around the city selling tickets; to the Heritage market by the docks, to Anfield on a matchday, in the middle of the city centre on Church Street even. We bought the car for about £7,500 and made about £16,000 on it.

The suggestions came rolling in. A promoter called Lyn Staunton and an agent called Malcolm Feld got in touch suggesting we arranged a concert. They came to see me bursting with ideas about acts and venues.

I decided to go for it and, with their backing, we approached the Empire. Within days we'd coughed up a £7,000 deposit to the Empire and booked it. I gave my own bank details and arranged for an overdraft.

We managed to pull off one of the best variety shows the Empire had ever seen. We got Gloria Gaynor to headline it, The Christians and Atomic Kitten re-formed, not to mention Pete Price, Billy Butler and a lot of other local comics. Tickets went like hot cakes. It was a sell-out and could've filled the place for four nights on the bounce.

The Empire show alone brought in about £60,000. Altogether, we raised £120,000 in three months.

It was a crazy time full of stress and sadness but also moments of laughter and excitement. The guy who had won the raffle for the car was in hospital when I phoned him, and he couldn't even remember buying a ticket. He was getting on a bit and wasn't interested.

"I don't want a car lad," he said. "Give it away."

I'd been buzzing when I phoned him to tell him he'd won, and had gathered everyone around me. We were all in stitches laughing. He came around to the idea in the end after we visited him in hospital and gave the car to his nephew.

During that time, I went to see Bishop of Liverpool James Jones up at his lodge in Woolton.

"I've been to see Michael and believe in him 100 per cent," I said. "I know it might be difficult for you to get involved, but is there anything you can do? The kid is in a desperate plight."

"Do you want me to go and see him?" he asked.

I was gobsmacked. Good to his word, he did, even going to see him three times in the UK after that first visit in Bulgaria. I know his prayers and support helped Michael.

I met with Jack Straw about four times, as we were building up our dossier of evidence which cleared Michael's name. At the same time, there was the evidence unearthed by the Trevor McDonald programme and the BBC Inside Out documentary which followed my meeting with Anthony Wilson and Bradley Thompson in a McDonald's restaurant in Liverpool.

We knew that Liverpool lads Wilson and Thompson were also there when Martin Georgiev was attacked and I decided to get them to tell the truth.

I'd got Thompson's number and arranged to meet them on the same day the then Home Secretary John Reid was in Garston.

I'd never met Thompson, so couldn't be sure who he was. I rang his phone and it rang out. He sat there eating a burger so I walked over and sat down.

"Thanks for agreeing to meet me," I said. Five minutes later, Anthony Wilson came in.

They insisted they weren't going to 'grass' on their mate, so I said I only wanted them to tell me what happened without throwing other names in. I work with young people every day and I'm used to that culture and attitude of not 'grassing'.

"I don't agree with your outlook, but I respect it," I said. "All

I'm asking you to do is tell me what went on. I want you to help Michael Shields because you know he wasn't there. Put yourself in his shoes.

"You'd hope someone would stand up for you."

They agreed to tell me, so we put together what had gone on without names. They both agreed with Ian's version of events. The bottom line was Michael was not there. When we'd finished talking, they promised to give me a written statement within days, but I waited for about a month with no contact.

Luckily I made notes of what was said straight after the meeting. I even told John Reid about it when I saw him later that day and he said he would help.

While I never heard from Thompson and Wilson again, Louise Ellman used her parliamentary privilege to raise it in the Commons. She named them both and told Government how they'd identified the real attacker and put Michael in the clear.

Shortly after that, I was leaving a meeting when I was threatened in a car park. I was walking to my car and a lad started shouting abuse at me.

Within minutes there were six of them glaring at me, shouting what they'd do to me if I wasn't careful. I considered stopping and going back but there was nothing I could have done against six lads. I got into my car and drove off. I found out later it was because of my role in the Shields campaign.

We pressed on. I took the dossier to Jack Straw's office with Bishop James in tow, but we couldn't get to see him. I'd been asking repeatedly to see Straw but it wasn't happening.

I was at the end of my tether. I rang Sheila Murphy, who was the regional director of the Labour party at the time.

"Look Sheila," I said. "I'm really fed up with this. There's an innocent man in jail and we have all this evidence. I'm sorry, but my own conscience and values are making me ashamed to be a member of the Labour party. I'm forever getting put off by Straw when I'm trying to make meetings.

"Now he says he can't see me for two weeks. These are days in that young boy's life. I'm resigning as leader from tomorrow. I'm going to call the group in and tell them tomorrow."

"Joe, you can't do that," she said.

"I'm sorry. You're not going to change my mind," I replied. "I've spoken to my wife about it and that's how I feel. I'll stay a member of the Labour party, but I won't have to be careful about what I say. I'll tell Jack Straw what I think."

Within 20 minutes Jack Straw was on the phone asking me not to resign. I remember distinctly what he said to me.

"Joe, if I had the authority to release him, I would."

This was a Sunday night and by the Tuesday I had a meeting with him. I went with Peter Weatherby and Louise Ellman.

I couldn't shake the thought that if this was someone in his own constituency, he'd be out already. I told him at that meeting to get Interpol or Merseyside Police to investigate the case. That's why it was doubly frustrating when he did that two years later. Why waste all that time?

It was to get worse. During the Royal Court of Justice hearing into whether Jack Straw could legally pardon Michael, the Government lawyers tried to discredit him. I was furious and cornered one of them during a break in proceedings.

"You're a disgrace," I said practically spitting out my words. "You represent a disgraceful Government and a minister who's behaved disgracefully. He's telling people that he supports Michael Shields, but then because you've lost this argument, he's trying to besmirch his name."

It was so uncomfortable watching the barrister on behalf of my party's Government assassinate Michael's character. I was sat squirming beside a coach-load of Michael's family and supporters. The argument Straw relied on – about this protocol for the transfer of prisoners abroad – has never been an issue for me. It's a simple issue about justice. Justice for an innocent man.

Our Government shouldn't have been predicating their stance on a possible future event like the transfer clause not working. The basic tenet of law should be about justice, not kowtowing to a state that wouldn't know justice if it bit them on the nose. It's a country that's so corrupt, the EU only allowed them in on the basis they change their legal system. I felt ashamed that our Government had acted so dishonourably. I was past caring, even if I was expelled as a party member. At least I could let rip then.

I've spoken to two prime ministers about the case, Tony Blair and Gordon Brown. Bulgarian politicians had told me they didn't care what the British Government did. They wouldn't hold a re-trial, but it was up to us. For the large part, the Government bottled it.

I've been to half a dozen prisons to visit Michael, driven countless miles, most of the time picking him up and then taking him back. Each time it's heartbreaking.

There have been times when Michael and I have cried together. I had to break the news to him about the European Court of Human Rights appeal failing. But it was also up to me to pick him up. To make him feel motivated again. I burned with the same frustration, the desire for our evidence to be heard. If you read it, saw it, tasted it, you just knew the kid was innocent. I felt like banging Jack Straw and Gordon Brown's heads together. "Why are you worried about upsetting someone else when you've got one of your own locked up?" I'd shout. The irony was that if he had committed the crime in this country, he would have been out by now. You can commit murder and be out in four years with mitigating circumstances.

At the same time my personal life was probably suffering. I wasn't spending as much time with my own four kids as I should have or my wife Marg. I was fortunate because my family were great. The staff at Chesterfield High School were brilliantly understanding. The Labour party in Liverpool were unflinching. Even the Bishop prayed for me.

I'd become so close to the Shields. At my 25th wedding anniversary party at the Devonshire Hotel in Liverpool, I asked people to make a donation to Michael's campaign instead of giving us gifts. We ended up with £2,000 on the night from cards.

I don't know how I managed at times; doing a full-time job leading the campaign on top of two other jobs, but I wouldn't change a thing.

It was the right thing to do.

12. Back On Home Ground

While I was adapting to life over there, my family were pulling up trees to get me transferred home.

Eventually, after a lot of arguing about how the fine I'd been given should be paid, their efforts paid off. I don't remember what day of the week it was when they told me I was going home, but I remember my bag was already half-packed, just in case.

Every day we'd be allowed outside from 12.30pm to 1.30pm, and that particular day, I could see cameras and TV crews outside the jail.

I knew there was no going back. As I went to find Ivan and say goodbye, one of the guards I got on well with stopped and asked if he could have a photograph taken with me. It was a nice gesture. We'd shared a lot of banter about footy.

It was not as emotional saying goodbye to Ivan as I'd thought it might have been. I knew I would end up speaking to him again one day anyway. He'd helped me an awful lot from day one in Varna jail and I was grateful.

"You've helped me so much and watched my back in here," I told him. "No matter what, I'll always help you when I get out. I'll have your back. If you come to the UK and need somewhere to stay, or anything, you only need to pick up the phone."

We shook hands and that was it. I was rushing around and my head was in a whirl. I was desperate to get out of there and now my moment had come. The guards checked my bag one final time and then gave me £50 in sterling, which I had to sign for.

I didn't glance back as I walked out of the prison entrance, under the huge stone archway and along the dry, dusty road.

I spotted a plain-clothes policeman with an earpiece standing at the side of the road and there were others standing nearby. 'What's the need for all this?' I thought. They ushered me into an unmarked car which was waiting with the engine running, and I had to sit in the middle of two policemen without a seat belt.

The driver was a lunatic, taking turns at high speed and roaring up and down busy streets on the way to the airport.

"If you slam on mate, I'm going flying through the windscreen," I said half-joking. He just nodded without smiling. I was thinking: 'I actually want to get home in one piece after all this.'

As we got to Varna airport, I could see more TV crews and reporters. 'I'll never have to see another Bulgarian TV camera again,' I thought. 'Thank God for that.'

I was led through the main departures area to a part which had been closed off just for me. Then two police officers took my fingerprints and checked my emergency passport. My real one had expired while I'd been in prison. I had to shake my head at the weirdness of the scene while we waited for the flight to be called.

On one side of the cordon were lots of ordinary, sun-tanned holidaymakers heading home after a fun-filled fortnight in Golden Sands or Sunny Beach. Then, on the other side of the cordon, was me – standing there in handcuffs looking sheepish, surrounded by 15 uniformed police officers.

I felt seriously self-conscious, as if all the holidaymakers were staring at me. A lot of them were. I hoped we weren't going to be standing here waiting too long.

Then two British police officers came over with the British consulate from Varna and his aide Daniella. As they introduced themselves, they pointed out our plane, which was landing.

Before long, I was on the coach on the way to the plane, still surrounded by officers and consular staff. I don't know what they were expecting. Some sort of last-minute prison break? I was going nowhere.

Did they think I wanted to run away and stay in Bulgaria? I'd have gladly let them put ankle shackles on me if it meant I could get out of that country more quickly.

When I get stressed, I tend to get tired, and I was feeling pretty stressed. I yawned. One of the British police officers started taking the piss a bit.

"Tired are we?" he asked. "Do you want to come back to the UK or what?" I just smiled and closed my eyes. Who cared what anyone said? I was on my way home.

I was led onto the plane and shown to a seat at the back in the corner. I had a police officer either side of me and then two in front. A few of the other regular passengers must have cottoned on to who I was and were looking over.

Journalist Andy Bonner was onboard the flight with a camera crew and he walked along the aisle to see if he could film me and grab a few words. Straight away one of the policemen stood up and said it was against Home Office protocol.

"If you film us, we will sue you," he said to Andy abruptly. I think he was camera shy. Andy couldn't exactly stand there arguing with him in the middle of the aisle so reluctantly he went back to his seat after we'd had a quick chat.

I was looking forward to a hot meal on the plane like the ones you get when you're going on your holidays. I'd pictured it for days. I should have known that hot meals and drinks didn't stretch to prisoner transfers. I got a cold chicken salad.

"Any chance of a drink?" I asked one of the policemen on the off-chance they'd say yes. "Maybe a beer?"

"You've got to be joking," he replied. I took that as a no. Instead, I closed my eyes again and pictured all the sky that was between us and Bulgaria. It felt good to be away from that country and heading home, even if the future was still so uncertain and still involved prison.

I woke up just before we were due to land at Gatwick, and once we'd touched down, I realised I'd have to wait until all the normal passengers got off. Instead of just letting me sit there, the police officers made me stand in the toilet. God knows why. It was pretty embarrassing having to hide myself away like that, but I just wanted to get off the plane.

Eventually, I was un-handcuffed and led off the plane to the empty tarmac below by two of the guards. It was not exactly the welcome home I'd wanted, but it would have to do. A sun-tanned policewoman came over to lead me to a waiting van.

"I'm going to have to put these cuffs back on you," she said.

As we pulled away from the airport, she was prattling on about the holiday in Goa, India, she'd just got back from. I was even more tired and when I'm knackered I can be a bit sarcastic. Again I thought it was best to bite my lip but I felt like saying, "I'm made-up you've had a good holiday. Mine was interesting, too. Wouldn't recommend Bulgaria, though."

I'd been told I might be taken to Wandsworth prison, but I was too young, so was bound for Feltham instead. It was the other side of London from Gatwick, so the journey took ages and, despite the lack of comfort, my head started to nod a bit.

CAMPAIGN GOES ON AS SHIELDS FLIES IN
By Kate Mansey

THE family of Michael Shields last night said they had "cleared a major hurdle" as their son arrived back in the UK.

Last night the Liverpool FC fan, who claims he was wrongly jailed in a Bulgarian prison, was flown home to continue his sentence in England.

The 20-year-old engineering student has spent the last 18 months incarcerated abroad after he was convicted for a crime he has always said he did not commit.

He was due to arrive at Heathrow airport at 8pm last night and will spend the next three to four weeks at Wandsworth Prison, London, which is the first port of call for all British nationals returning from foreign jails.

At Wandsworth, he will be assessed before being moved to another UK prison. It will be the first time he has been on British soil since leaving Wavertree to watch Liverpool FC play in the Champions League final in May 2005.

Yesterday, Michael Shields' family and friends spoke of their relief at his return.

His aunt Jeanette Shields, 48, said: "When his plane touches down, we'll jump up with joy.

"It is a brilliant day – we're ecstatic. We're not celebrating exactly because we're all still in shock. We just can't wait to see him.

"We've had so many ups and downs in the past 18 months. We've climbed so many hurdles and we've fallen flat a few times, but we're looking to the future now and we'll keep on climbing."

His mother Maria paid one final visit to her son in Varna prison before the news came that he would be coming home.

She said: "Michael has no idea what it will be like inside a British prison because he's never set foot in one.

"But, more than anything, he's just glad to be going home.

"When I was leaving, some of his friends in the prison came and shook my hand and the jail social worker said he is a lovely lad and she'll miss him.

"Michael said he can't wait to see his nan when he gets back. She hasn't been well and it's been worrying him."

Father Michael Snr added: "I'm full of mixed emotions. I'm full of joy that he will be in his own country and we won't have to be travelling and banging our heads against a brick wall with the Bulgarians.

"The past 18 months have been the worst of our lives – just so exhausting and now we can try and get some normality back. But I'm sad that he has to come home and then go into a prison cell because he's an innocent lad."

Last night, politicians vowed to continue the fight which will go all the way to the European Court of Human Rights.

Yesterday morning, Arlene McCarthy, Euro MP for the North West, met with the Bulgarian Chief Prosecutor, who was responsible for signing Michael Shields' transfer papers to the UK, to discuss the next steps. Ms McCarthy said: "This will be a tremendous boost to both Michael personally and his family, although he is not yet back home with his family.

"Since his trial and subsequent appeals, his family have been through hell and I welcome the fact that he has been transferred back to the UK. After 18 months' incarceration in a Bulgarian jail, our first priority now has to be Michael's psychological and physical welfare."

Cllr Joe Anderson, who has been instrumental in the Shields campaign, said: "It's absolutely brilliant news. By getting him out of Bulgaria, we've completed the first part of the race. Now we'll continue to fight to prove his innocence."

Speaking from Westminster, Louise Ellman, MP for Riverside, Liverpool, said: "I'm delighted that he is now back in the UK. It's what Michael and his family wanted.

"We've all campaigned hard for this and I've raised this repeatedly with ministers in Parliament, but we must continue the campaign for justice and I will continue to work with Michael, his family and his legal team to make sure that happens."

The transfer follows months of negotiations with officials in Bulgaria, where Shields has been held since a 10-year sentence was passed over the alleged attempted murder of a barman. The next stage of the process will see him take the fight to the European Court of Human Rights, where his lawyers will argue that he did not receive a fair trial.

– Liverpool Daily Post, November 24, 2006

My first night in Feltham, a Thursday, was spent on an observation wing. The beds were more comfortable than anything I'd rested my head on for the last year-and-a-half, and even though I automatically checked under the mattress and behind the curtains, I was pretty sure there would be no cockroaches.

One of the doctors asked me a few questions and they did a few basic tests to check how healthy I was, but I'd already been told I was moving again the next morning. Next stop was further north, up to Hindley.

After a quiet first day in Hindley, when I went through what was to become a repeated feeling of first-day nerves multiplied by 100, I got some good news.

One of the people I'd missed most while I was in Bulgaria was my nan, or 'Minty', and she was going to be visiting me on Saturday morning with my mum and dad.

She was 76 and I hadn't seen her in over a year-and-a-half. I knew she'd been worried sick about me, and she'd sent loads of cards and letters while I was in Bulgaria.

I was happy to see her, but it was so different seeing her in that context of prison, and I was still coming to terms with the new environment myself. She was great because she didn't get too upset and I was really upbeat afterwards.

What I didn't know was that she was in tears on the way home from Hindley afterwards. She said she was so relieved I was home but shocked at the weight I'd lost and having to see me in a prison. It wasn't easy for any of my family seeing me like that.

At least now we were in the same country she could come and see me more often.

13. No Rights

I got to Hindley young offenders centre on a Friday, and had to adjust quickly over the weekend.

When prisoners first get to a jail in the UK, it's called 'landing'. I landed at Hindley at the same time as a few Manc lads, so straight away I was looking for any Scousers to fit in with.

I was expecting something like out of the film 'Scum', a place full of random violence and unpredictable head-cases. I was expecting to be forced to join some mad gang or something.

"When you go for your dinner, go to the two furthest tables in the dining room," one lad told me.

It sort of confirmed what I was worried about. That there was going to be these gangs at war in the prisons.

It actually wasn't that bad, though. If anything, when a new lad lands, the others try and look out for them. You get given a bag from the other lads which has got stuff like shower gel and deodorant in. Even biscuits. It's a solidarity thing, really. "We're all in this boat together." That's not to say it's all smiles all the time, but it was a better start than I expected.

At night you tended to go down from your pad onto the association where you might play pool.

At Hindley, I got to know a lad really well who was my age and in for armed robbery. He was from Dingle in Liverpool, and it was good to speak to another lad who hadn't grown up a million miles from me. We had a fair bit in common.

I was in Hindley with him from 2006 and later on he was even up in Warrington with me. It was funny how it came full circle.

The majority of lads in a prison you don't become mates with. You let onto them and say alright, but not mates. So then when I saw him in Warrington I was made up. Even though he was put on a different wing, we could catch up.

It's funny because before all this happened, I would never have had a clue about all the ins and outs of armed robbery or selling drugs, but I wasn't naive. I mean, I was streetwise. You can't grow up in Liverpool and be totally naive, but I wasn't knocking about with bad lads.

I've always tried to learn from the lads I've met inside. Learn in a positive way.

This one lad had been locked up for hitting another fella during an argument in a club. They'd both been drunk and he was scared he was going to get battered by the other fella who was bigger and stronger-looking than him.

He'd punched him once and the other bloke fell back and hit his head. It had left him on a life-support machine.

"If you ever end up in this situation, just walk away lad," he said to me. "Making the wrong decision and throwing one punch cost me 14 years. It's not worth it. Now I've got this stigma with me forever... what I did."

I already knew that your life can change in an instant. The time it takes for something awful to happen. My life changed the time it took someone else to do something horrible, but I knew the lesson was still important.

It has felt like a lifetime for me in many ways, but it has only been four years. People like this lad were looking at being away for 14 years.

Later, when I was moved to an adult jail, I realised there are a lot of people who are inside for killing their wives or girlfriends. You wouldn't believe the amount of people who snap and do that. A lot of them aren't people who are made for prison life. They're successful people who should be living in a big house somewhere posh. If I saw a fight in jail, I wouldn't think it was the end of the world, but some of these men would be mortified.

They are middle class and have grown up in a cocoon when it comes to some of the darker things in life.

They moan over every little thing inside. If an officer opens the door five minutes late or something, they moan. Even though they're in prison, they can't adapt.

If there is a big fight on one of the wings and the guards go around asking if people saw anything, you know what to say.

"Sorry Guv, I didn't see anything. Can't help."

You see these fellas, though, and they're blabbing away telling the guards every last detail. "…And then this lad ran around and did this while this other lad was hanging around his neck and throwing punches."

You cringe for them because it's not the way to get by. These are men in their 30s and 40s who should be outside cleaning their Jaguars.

In Thorn Cross, Warrington, I'd meet lads who only come in for a month. They come in straight off the street and they've got this bad attitude. You see them come in, and me and my mates laugh.

We just keep our heads down and don't bother anyone.

These new lads walk around with their chests out, staring at other lads trying to look hard and I'll say to one of the lads:

"He wouldn't last five minutes in Garth. He'd get killed."

That is what lads must be like when they go into somewhere like Walton.

Or you'll get lads who'll say: "I've been in for two months and got another one to go before I get off on a tag. My head's battered. I hate it."

Straight-faced, I'd say: "I've been in for four years, you know, and I've got a year left. You want to try that."

"I'm sorry," they'll say, thinking I'm serious, but I'm only winding them up. Everyone's own problems are the biggest thing for them.

I always tried to keep myself to myself. I've just found that was the best way. If someone came over to me and wanted to ask about the case, I don't really want to know. I will just answer politely, but keep it to yes or no. I don't really speak to strangers. Only lads I can trust. Only the good lads I've latched onto. I've made some good mates in prison, though. To me the scariest thing is that for some people I've met, five years is nothing. It's just the start of their sentence.

One lad I still write to is in for 16 years and he looks no different from anyone else. I met him in Garth and he's the sort of lad you could easily picture just going to university or chatting to about football in a bar, but he's not, he's in a prison. He was done on a murder charge.

His family is from Heswall in Wirral but he's not spoilt. They are originally from Tuebrook and they've made their money and moved away. He's still one of the lads, but he's from a rich background.

We used to joke and call him 'American Psycho' after the character Christian Bale played in the film. If you walk in his cell, it's like an Albert Dock flat. He's got black and white prints on the wall and everything is trendy and immaculate.

I remember one time I got a picture postcard of Marilyn Monroe, a black and white one. I knew straight away he'd like it, so I cut it carefully down the middle and kept the bit with the message on.

"I've got a present for you," I said after knocking on his pad door.

He was delighted. "It's brilliant," he said. "It'll go perfectly over there."

The next day it was positioned perfectly on the wall of his pad. He even makes you take your trainers off when you go in his pad. He walks around the wing in his flip-flops with a spiky, gelled hairstyle carrying a cup of tea. You just wouldn't picture him in prison if you met him. He just accepts his sentence.

"What's done is done. I've just got to get on with it," he says.

I latched onto him because he's a big Evertonian and loves his football. We can have proper banter about the Reds and the Blues. With some of the lads who tend to hang around in gangs, it's like you've heard the same conversation about what they used to get up to outside a thousand times.

It was in May 2007, the day United got beat by AC Milan away that we finally got the knockback from the European Court of Human Rights.

It was an unscheduled Wednesday night visit from Joe Anderson, so I knew it had to be about something important. I remember he told me straight. I'd become very close to Joe and can never thank him enough for all his support. I wouldn't have wanted to hear news, good or bad, from anyone else.

"That's it then," I thought. "It's over." It still pisses me off when I see a newspaper article about human rights.

That night I came as close as I've ever been to giving up.

"Joe, let's forget about it," I said. "Fuck them. The Bulgarians, the European Parliament, our Government. Fuck them all. I've had enough. I can't be bothered banging my head against a brick wall anymore.

"Tell my mum and dad to forget about it. I'm tired of fighting it and getting knocked back every time. I'll just try and move through the system. See out my sentence."

Joe was having none of it. "You don't mean that," he said. "You're entitled to feel let down and fed up, but you're not going to give in. None of us are.

"We've come this far. You're back home and even though we've had another setback, we're not stopping. You're going to get out of prison and get your life back. I promise you that. Anyway, I've already promised your mother and I'm not letting her down either."

Joe's words lifted me up. As much as I wanted to abandon the ups and downs of fighting the case, I knew I couldn't give in.

The anger and bitterness I felt wasn't going to get the better of me. The corrupt police in Bulgaria, the judges, then the politicians in the UK who kept me in prison. They weren't going to beat me.

HEARTBREAK AS EURO JUDGES REJECT APPEAL
Exclusive By Greg O'Keeffe

MICHAEL Shields' hopes of clearing his name were shattered by European judges today.

The Liverpool fan's case for an appeal against his conviction for attempted murder was rejected by the European Court of Human Rights in Strasbourg.

Three judges ruled Michael's rights were not violated during his trial and conviction in Bulgaria.

The decision comes almost two years after the 20-year-old Reds fan was convicted in Bulgaria of seriously injuring a barman after Liverpool's 2005 Champions League final win.

The former engineering student was moved from Bulgaria to a prison cell in Wigan last year.

His mother Maria was today bed-ridden with stress after hearing the news.

His tearful father Michael Snr, a window cleaner from Edge Hill, said: "I am heartbroken. It is hard to find the words to say how low we are.

"We have waited two years for the European court to turn around and kick us in the teeth.

"It's hard to see where we will turn next, but we will fight on for Michael. My wife is in bed devastated and my girls are just crying constantly."

The court's decision by judges from Spain, Macedonia and Liechtenstein was sent by letter to Michael's solicitor John Weate, of RMNJ (Roberts Moore Nicholas, Jones), in Wirral.

Michael's campaign team, led by city Labour leader Joe Anderson and MP Louise Ellman, had hoped the court would consider deep flaws in the identification process which led to the conviction.

As the Echo revealed first in May 2005:

* Bulgarian police left him handcuffed to a radiator in a room where witnesses taking part in the ID parade passed through.

* He was forced to wear clothes in an identity parade he did not wear on the night of the assault.

Cllr Anderson, who broke the news to Michael during a visit last night, said: "It's a huge setback. Probably the darkest hour in our fight for justice.

"But this means now, more than ever, those who witnessed the attack in Golden Sands and know what really happened must come forward.

"We have to appeal to them and their families to look at their consciences and ask if they can now let an innocent man stay in jail for the rest of his sentence.

"The people of this city know who these witnesses are.

They should now do the right thing once and for all."

Cllr Anderson, who helped organise the Empire concert which raised £90,000 to pay Michael's fine from the Bulgarian courts, called on Echo readers to sign the petition he has placed on the Downing Street website.

"The fight continues. I remain absolutely 110% convinced of Michael's innocence. I would like everyone to sign the petition which is on the No 10 Downing Street website. That calls for the Bulgarians to allow Interpol to interview new witnesses which the appeal courts in both Bulgaria and now Strasbourg have ignored."

Mrs Ellman said: "I am deeply disappointed and I will be discussing the situation with Michael's legal team and family to see what can be done next.

"We will continue to fight for justice for Michael. He is an innocent young man who has been treated very badly throughout."

– Liverpool Echo, May 3, 2007

I still couldn't believe they basically said that the charade, the show trial, which I'd had in Bulgaria, wasn't a breach of my human rights.

How could they sit there and say I'd had the right to a fair trial? My legal team had given them more than enough evidence that it was about as far away from fair as you could get.

There just seemed to be no sense to it. It was even worse that they didn't consider my case. They actually ruled that it was not worth considering because there'd been no breach.

I picked up a newspaper once to see that they heard a case from a man who wanted to disprove God. I was stunned. They had time to consider some nonsense like that, but not a single moment for me.

I'd had it drummed into me to expect an impartial and fair hearing, so I allowed myself a bit of hope, but they knocked it back at the first hurdle. They turned around and said no without even giving me a reason why.

Surely it's a human right to know why they didn't consider it?

Not even my barrister Peter Weatherby or the Euro MP Arlene McCarthy could find out their reason.

To make things even more infuriating, the European Parliament actually backed my case after a speech from Arlene. They were politicians, not judges or lawyers, and they could see the problems, so how could the legal experts not? I wonder if it was simply because Bulgaria were on the brink of membership into the EU and to say their legal system was faulty would be undermining them.

Two years after that amazing night in Istanbul, Liverpool got through to another European Cup final. Once again the opponents were AC Milan and this time the game was played in the ancient Greek capital, Athens.

A lot of people have asked if it upset me that another final had come around and I couldn't go. In many ways it seemed like a carbon copy of Istanbul.

I suppose they thought that it would bring all the negative memories of the trip to Bulgaria flooding back.

It was actually the opposite.

I was just as excited as any other Liverpool fan and the only thing which depressed me was when they lost. A lot of my mates in there used to say they couldn't get over how much I still loved Liverpool.

"I'd never go the match again if I was you," said one lad.

But I was just drawn back into it.

Liverpool are in my blood and always will be. It wasn't the club's fault this had happened to me. If anything, they'd done everything they could to help.

The first time I saw a mosaic on the Kop supporting my case will never leave me. It was while I was still in Bulgaria and we were playing Sunderland.

At first I couldn't figure out what it was that the cameras kept panning to during the game.

Then it hit home.

"Me," I said pointing to the screen and trying to make my Bulgarian pad-mate understand.

"Liverpool fans are for me," I repeated.

He didn't seem to fully understand, but he knew the mosaic was about me. It was surreal, but it gave me a real boost knowing there were lads back home, sitting in Anfield watching the match and thinking of me.

I've always put Liverpool pictures up in the different cells I've been in. The one that means the most to me is Jamie Carragher celebrating on the pitch after we'd won the European Cup. His arms are in the air and it summed up the joy of that night perfectly.

In the UK, I used to go into my cell and listen to every game on the radio. I remember in the run-up to the 2007 Athens final when we played Barcelona and it was 0-1 after Deco had scored.

I was gutted, but we came back and won 2-1 and I was dancing around. I was allowed to watch the semi-final against Chelsea and I'll never forget how nervous I was.

One of my mates in Hindley was from Manchester and he was giving me a bit of stick when we were beaten that night. Not just me, he was dishing it out to another lad, an Everton fan, who'd stuck up for Liverpool in the final even though he was a bitter Blue.

I had to wait a while to get my own back, but the chance came big time when United were totally outclassed by Barcelona in Rome in the Champions League final this year. He definitely heard me when Barcelona won. He heard me when Everton beat United in the FA Cup semi-final, too.

14. UK Time

On the first Sunday at Hindley, my mates Danny, Mark and Paul came up to see me. They weren't with me in Istanbul – two of them are Blues – but I've grown up with them.

I told them all about the difference between Bulgaria and UK prisons, like how I could get the Liverpool station Radio City on the little radio in my cell and listen to the footy.

It was good being back in the North West, at least. A visit in Bulgaria is on a different, much smaller scale, and you can only speak through a phone either side of a glass window.

In Hindley, there was a massive visiting room with lots of tables in it. You can hear what people to the side of you and behind you are saying, which isn't ideal, and you have to wear your prison uniform of jeans and a proper convict-style blue and white striped T-shirt, too.

I hate dressing in prison clothes. The rest of the time on the wing you got given a tracksuit to wear. We all hated them because they were the same colour as corned-beef. Later, when I was moved to Garth, it was all the wrong-uns, the sex offenders and weirdos, who wore the corned-beef trackies. Thankfully, we got something different to wear.

No matter what they give you to wear in prison, it'll never fit anyway. I've never been given a pair of jeans which even remotely fit. You are always walking to your visit trying to hold your jeans up with one hand, or having to breathe in because they are so tight. In a way, that's good, because you don't ever want to get comfortable in prison clothes. In that way, I'm happy they never fit.

If the clothes are bad, though, the food in British prisons is even worse.

The Government seems to always be announcing the importance of healthy eating and getting your five portions of fruit a day, but that doesn't stretch to the jails. You haven't got a hope in hell of getting five bits of fruit a day.

In the morning, they usually put a box of oranges on the wing, and you can grab one of them, but that's it. When you are having your lunch, there may be vegetables, but most of the time they're tasteless mush.

They give us chips every day, too, which isn't great if you're trying to get in shape. I remember once I asked about healthier food when it was getting towards summer.

"Is there any chance of getting the odd salad as we get into summer, Miss?" I asked one of the female governors. "It'd be cheaper and easier for them to do."

"No," she said, not very impressed by my attempt at playing the health card. "You're a minority and everyone else wants chips."

"Yeah but not everyone wants to be fat," I said. She was having none of it and there was no point arguing. The sausages, chips, tripe and bad burgers would continue.

It was only later when I'd get out on licence that I realised what proper food is like again. I had a jacket potato when I was at my sister Melissa's house one night and it was lovely. It was like a totally different food from the rock-solid ones you get in prison.

Once, we were sat having our lunch and one of the lads was sawing into his jacket spud, taking ages because of the rock-hard skin, and when he finally cracked it, he found a worm waiting for him. It was the last time any of us at that table ate our jacket potato in prison.

The burgers were atrocious, too. They were more ground-up fat than meat. I've only ever eaten one stew in prison, a vegetarian one in Garth, as everywhere else they just put tripe in it because it's so cheap.

You'd spend most of your time picking pigs' stomachs out of your dish. Even basic meals where you'd think they couldn't go wrong, like stuffed peppers or tuna pasta, could somehow be messed up in prison.

I remember when one of the cooks got punched. He was knocked out cold. They never caught who did it, but he'd probably had enough of cold tripe stew and snapped. I wouldn't have been surprised if the governor had seen it and turned a blind eye. The food really is that bad!

I'm a major tea-tank. We are allowed to order tea and coffee to our wings once a week and I'll have maybe four cups of tea a day and five at night. I can't go without my PG Tips. There's a hot water boiler on the ground floor of the wing and you go and fill your flask up.

I remember at Haverigg jail we all had a sneaky stash of George Foreman grills. We weren't strictly allowed them, but as soon as the screws would turn their backs, we'd have our George Foreman grills out. We soon learned you can cook anything on a George Foreman.

Not just the usual bacon or sausage, but also omelettes and French toast. We had to be creative because the food in Haverigg was particularly bad.

One day I was working in the library, so I went into the kitchen to bring one of the chefs a newspaper, and the things I saw in there scarred me for life. I think you had to have problems to work in those kitchens. I saw one of them making himself a sandwich and it was bizarre.

He just emptied a whole jar of paprika onto a piece of bread, made a sandwich of it and tucked in.

Elsewhere, there would be two of them hanging over a big vat of curry, stirring it. "They could do anything they want to that," I thought. It's why I've never eaten anything with sauces on it in prisons. I just stick to brown or red sauce. Best to be on the safe side.

It's at special times throughout the year when the food situation hits the hardest.

Christmas Day 2005 in Bulgaria, we got a chicken leg and boiled rice for tea. I was dreaming about my mum's roast turkey with stuffing and all the trimmings, and there I was with this little bowl of rice and a skinny chicken leg. I think I knocked myself up a salad for a starter and then phoned home almost in tears.

Over here it's a bit different on Christmas Day. People understandably get annoyed when they hear of prisoners getting a proper Christmas dinner or Christmas pudding, but they don't have to taste them. They wouldn't get so worked up if they did.

People don't moan too much about the Christmas food in jail, because at that time, especially, you don't like to be reminded of what you're missing.

Moaners get given a wide berth. You might give them sympathy the first time they complain, perhaps they're worried that their girlfriend is cheating on them, but if they bang on about it for weeks, they soon lose everyone's interest.

You hear them on the phone to their girlfriend and they will say halfway through a conversation: "Tell that lad to get out of the wardrobe," trying to catch them out.

They are only doubling their sentence by worrying, though. I've always said they should get rid of them if they don't trust them.

I went through a very low period as my 21st birthday

approached on September 21, 2007. I knew that once I'd turned 21, I would probably be sent to adult prison for the first time, and I was dreading it.

My mind had been put at ease by the governor at Hindley, though, who'd assured me that I'd be kept there for nine months after my 21st. The logic was that I could finish an education course I'd been doing, so I'd told my family I'd be able to stay for the time being.

I was settled there and as happy as I could be, heading towards category C prisoner status which would've meant my next jail would be more relaxed.

I'd already decided to blank out of my mind any thoughts that I should be going out with my mates or having a big family meal to celebrate my birthday. When I was 18, I remember having a meal with my mum and dad, but no party. Back then, I was very shy and hated the idea of being the centre of attention. I was happy to just hang out with my mates on the street. In hindsight, I wished I'd had a big party and celebrated the last landmark birthday before I was locked up.

When it came, my 21st was just a normal day for me, although perhaps less so for the other prisoners.

They would switch the TV on and see my family releasing balloons outside the prison and holding up banners. Even in the weeks before, the publicity about my birthday meant I was coming back to my pad from working and getting huge stacks of birthday cards.

I was really pleased, but embarrassed at the same time. It's hard to be down when strangers are sending you birthday cards wishing you good luck. It was just the same old slop for tea on the night of my 21st itself and the only high point was a visit from my family in the evening. Luckily my parents and sisters came with my niece and nephew.

The message from my family was the same as it had been for the last four years.

"This is your first and last Christmas in prison," they'd say, or: "You won't have to spend another birthday behind bars."

They said it with the best intentions to cheer me up, but I believed them less and less every time.

With the European Court of Human Rights, I'd really believed they would help me. I expected nothing better than I got towards the end of my time in Bulgaria, but the European decision gutted us.

I SHOULD BE ENJOYING MY 21ST BIRTHDAY
INSTEAD OF BEING STUCK IN HERE
By Greg O'Keeffe

JAILED Liverpool fan Michael Shields today spoke of how he should be celebrating his landmark 21st birthday with the people he loves.

Instead, the engineering student was spending today alone in his cell at Hindley jail near Wigan with only an evening family visit to look forward to.

Speaking from jail last night, he said: "My 21st will be like the last two Christmas Days I've been in jail. I just want to get them out of the way so I'm a day nearer to getting out. It will just be another 24 hours when I'm in here and the world carries on. I should be celebrating with my family and friends instead of stuck in here."

Michael's sisters Laura and Melissa were due to visit him tonight with his niece Kelsy and nephew Philip. His parents Michael Snr and Maria will see him tomorrow. They are restricted in what gifts they can take.

Instead, they will deliver scores of cards well-wishers have posted to their home in Edge Hill along with two from Liverpool stars Jamie Carragher and Steven Gerrard.

Inside his card, Carragher has written: "To Michael, Happy

21st mate. Keep going – you are not forgotten."

Michael's father said: "Maria and I feel heartbroken Michael isn't with us for his big day. It's horrible to think it will just be a routine day. You only turn 21 once and my son is doing it as an innocent person behind bars.

"When he was 18, he didn't want a party, but he always said he'd have a 21st with his mate Paul Kelly who shares his birthday. Paul isn't going to have a party now because he's too sad. He's going to wait until Michael gets out."

A petition on the prime minister's website calling for Michael to be freed is already one of the most strongly supported in the country, having amassed more than 15,000 signatures.

But Cllr Joe Anderson, leading the fight to see Michael released, has his sights firmly set on the 100,000 mark.

He said: "I'd like to urge everyone who has supported Michael so loyally so far to go online and sign the petition. We won't give in."

– Liverpool Echo, September 21, 2007

It was a few days after my 21st that I was hit with more crushing news. I was getting some hot water for my cup of tea one evening, and opened the cell door to find three screws standing there.

"We're going to get spun here," I said to my pad-mate, meaning they looked like they were ready to search the cell. Instead, the most senior screw threw a bag at me.

"Get packed," he said. "You're going to Garth in the morning." I started to laugh. "What?" I said sitting down on my bed. "I don't even know anyone in Garth. It's an adult prison."

My pad-mate looked gutted, too. We got on well. What pissed me off even more was that the screws had seen me on the phone earlier to my mum and dad. They didn't even give me the chance to tell them I was being moved. There are a lot of people on power trips in prison. Men who love all the rules and regulations and relish the control they have over the prisoners.

"I don't suppose there's a chance I can phone my mum back and tell her I'm getting moved?" I asked the senior screw, knowing what his answer would be.

"You're mad aren't you?" he said and closed the door.

Garth was a category B prison and there'd be lads doing some serious stretches in there. Mine would be one of the shorter sentences. I was walking around my pad gathering what little stuff I had, thinking: 'What if there's going to be a dick-head who wants to try and do me in?' I didn't even know anyone who'd been in Garth.

"I've been in worse places," I said to my pad-mate. "I suppose I'm going to have to get on with it now. No point stressing."

"I bet they put some little wrong 'un in here with me now," he said, still looking devastated. It was another of many sleepless nights. The next day I got up with my bags packed and most of the lads had gone off to their different prison jobs.

They left my pad door open as the cleaners were doing the wing and I walked around saying my goodbyes to the few lads who weren't working. Another one of the lads on the wing was being taken to Wymott, which is near Garth, and we were chatting as we waited for the sweat-box to pick us up. The sweat-box is what we called the claustrophobic transport vans with blacked out windows we'd be taken in between jails.

"Good luck for the future," said one of the senior officers, but I didn't want to know.

'I haven't got much of a future in Garth,' I thought. On the way, we were winding each other up to break the tension.

"You want to stay away from all the sex offenders on the Dark Side in Wymott," I was saying.

"You'll have to mingle with all the lifers in Garth," he fired back. On the way we picked up four other prisoners who were going to a lower category prison and they were discussing their day release visits and all the plans they had.

'That's a world away from what I'm going to,' I thought, getting more and more downhearted despite the banter. We went past Wymott before we went to Garth and it looked OK, with a fence and not a wall. Then we got to Garth and saw a huge, intimidating wall and the big bleak building.

"Yours looked nice but I don't know about mine," I said to my mate.

"I know," he said, looking it up and down.

The sweat-box stopped and the driver turned to us. "I hate dropping people off here," he said. "It's always too quiet."

"That can't be a bad thing, surely?" I said.

"I don't know," he replied. "It's full of weirdos."

'Great. Thanks for that,' I thought. 'I'm only 21. You've cheered me up there.'

MICHAEL SHOCK AS HE'S
MOVED TO ADULT PRISON
By Greg O'Keeffe

MICHAEL SHIELDS was today moved to an adult prison for the first time in the UK.

He was transferred from Hindley young offenders prison in Wigan to the category B Garth jail in Preston where he will be among criminals serving life sentences.

Today his parents told of their shock at the speed of the move, only days after he turned 21.

His father Michael Snr said: "We knew he'd be moving to an adult prison eventually, but the speed at which it happened has shocked us.

"My wife has been in tears because the reality of it is hitting home now. Michael will be in a normal prison like Walton now, with proper hardened criminals.

"We didn't know until only a few hours before the transfer. He's just going to keep his head down now and get back to his studies."

Liverpool Labour party leader Joe Anderson, who is leading the campaign to free Michael, said: "We had hoped Michael could stay at Hindley longer to continue the good education he started there.

"Instead we'll continue our fight to have him moved to an open prison as soon as possible. I hope the news of how long Michael has to serve embarrasses the real culprits and their families who know the truth about what happened in Bulgaria.

"Maybe their consciences will finally persuade them to come forward."

Yesterday the Echo revealed how the Edge Hill student's provisional release date, conditional on good behaviour, is May 30, 2010.

The date was agreed by law and order minister David Hanson after a legal wrangle.

It is 10 months earlier than the tariff first set by the Home Office under rules which did not fully take account of the time Michael spent in Bulgarian custody before he was convicted of an assault on a barman.

But the Whitehall interpretation of those rules was challenged by Michael's lawyer John Weate, of Birkenhead firm RMN&J.

The Home Office has now agreed he should be released after serving half of his reduced 10-year sentence, including pre-trial custody.

– Liverpool Echo, September 26, 2007

Garth was another maze of corridors and I'd be there over the winter. Everywhere you walked, it was just corridor after corridor.

One of the guards greeted me with a trolley and told me to put my bags in it and follow him. I must have looked puzzled, because normally prisoners are made to carry their own bags, and taking the inconvenience away from them would hardly be a consideration.

"You'll see why," said the guard smiling. We embarked on a 10-minute walk through more and more corridors until we arrived at my wing.

It was the first proper prison wing I'd been on in terms of its three-floor stacked layout with only metal grill flooring between each level. Bulgarian jails were much different and Hindley had been set out more like flats. Garth was like an old-school prison.

"Big, isn't it?" I muttered to nobody in particular. At least it looked clean. Immediately I felt lonely again as I took in the scale of the place. Again, I started listening out for lads from Liverpool. You'll always get people who will come over and say: "You're that kid who was locked up in Bulgaria aren't you? Are you getting out?"

"You know more than me," was always my stock response. I never wanted to talk about it to strangers and was always wary of someone thinking they could make a name for themselves by having a go at me.

As I stood by the entrance to my single-bed cell, a lad came over.

"What's happenin' mate?" he said in a broad Scouse accent. "How are you? Come down onto the landing later and have a game of pool with us."

It was a nice gesture and made me feel that tiny bit less lonely. I used the phone to tell my mum and dad where I was and then went and leaned over the railing looking down at the different prisoners mingling, talking, arguing. Soon I saw the lad who had asked me to play pool turn up with some others and begin a game.

I went down and the other lads were equally friendly. It turned out they were all Scousers and we got on well. It was a huge relief. Now, if I was waiting in the dinner queue, I could go and stand with them, or if I was bored, there would be someone to play pool or cards with. They became firm friends who I spent most of my time in Garth with. I'm still in touch with some of them now.

My mood improved even more when I realised there were more channels on the TVs in our room, including Sky Sports News. I'd be able to keep up to date with Liverpool now without having to constantly ask people.

It was a nice novelty being able to watch it during quiet time when you've got to stay in your cell, known as 'bang-up'. Even the food was slightly better than Hindley, although it couldn't be much worse.

I was there during the winter, so it was always pretty gloomy outside. We were allowed an hour's outdoor exercise a day but it was normally freezing in the yard and I had no coat, just my prison greys. It's like one of the wind-ups we went on to play on other new boys after I'd fitted into the crowd.

"Haven't you got a coat?" we'd ask. "Go and ask the screw for a big, warm coat." They'd trot over and ask the screw and get laughed at. Prisons don't provide big warm coats.

It's like once we were in the prison gym and saw a new lad watching himself shadow box in a mirror.

He was deliberately throwing combinations of air punches, bobbing and weaving like he was preparing for a fight in the ring. Joe Calzaghe eat your heart out.

"We'll have to reel him in a bit," said one of the lads, laughing.

"Listen mate," said another when the wannabe champ had finished trying to act tough. "Why don't you go and ask that screw over there if you can get your name onto the list for this weekend?"

"What's happening this weekend?" asked the boxer, suddenly interested.

"We're going swimming," said my mate. "It's a great weekend. The guards take us off to a local swimming baths and we stay overnight in a hotel nearby. We're even allowed a little drink after."

We forced our faces to remain sincere until he'd turned around and hot-footed it off to find a screw. Then we burst into howls of laughter. We were still in stitches when he came back 10 minutes later looking sheepish. He laughed about it in the end and it's happened to us all.

If a newcomer complains about the food, someone will tell him to go and ask the kitchen for a special sandwich bag from Marks & Spencer. You'd be amazed how many fall for it.

Practical jokes help you get through the boredom and misery of prison.

In Garth, you had your ID card on the wall outside your cell with name, number and a picture, and it's laminated. Me and some of the lads used to get some of the strands from an old mop and stick them onto the pictures so it looked like a droopy moustache or crazy hairdo. People would come back from work and see their photos had been altered.

You had to find ways to keep laughing to stop yourself going mad or getting depressed.

Simple as that.

15. Bulgarian Breakthrough

Joe Anderson explained to me during a phone call that he'd been in touch with a polygraph expert who had agreed to carry out a test for me.

We'd spoken a few times about me taking a lie detector test, but the biggest stumbling block had always been whether we'd get permission from the prison.

Well, somehow Joe and my legal team had persuaded the prison service to let me take the test.

I'd always said I'd take one in an instant to prove I had nothing to do with it. Anything which would add credibility to our campaign could only be a good thing.

But at the same time, I began to worry. I knew I was innocent, but what if the machine went wrong for some reason?

What if, despite answering the questions honestly, I got really nervous and my nerves affected the reading? Thinking about the test was a vicious circle and made me more nervous about it.

When the day came, my stomach was churning. Nobody could be in the room with me apart from the British Polygraphers' Association examiner Don Cargill and the machine.

Before I went in, I had to answer some questions from a forensic psychologist called Dr Keith Ashcroft to see if I was in the right state of mind to be tested. Shortly after, he confirmed I was OK and that was it.

Joe and I sat beside each other outside the test room. If I had been nervous before taking my driving test, this was a million times worse. The governor of Garth prison was hovering around, too.

"You'll be OK, lad," said Joe, trying to calm me down. "You've got nothing to worry about. You're just telling the truth."

"What if it goes wrong?" I said. I'd thought the truth would save me before and it hadn't. There was no backing out, though. I was just going to get it over with.

The setup in the room was like something out of a film about the FBI. Just a desk with the machine on it and two chairs.

I had to wear a strap around my arm to monitor my pulse and another wire was attached to my chest to watch my heart rate. They were even monitoring my sweat and breathing.

The questions began.

"Were you involved on the attack on Martin Georgiev?" asked Mr Cargill.

"No," I replied. I felt suddenly calm after answering the main question. I was telling the truth and that was all I could do.

"Were you in the area when Martin Georgiev was attacked?" he continued.

"No," I replied again, my voice firm.

The questions carried on coming until two hours had passed and the test was over. The monitors were taken off and I was able to leave.

"How long until I get to know the results," I asked.

"It won't be immediate, unfortunately," said Mr Cargill. "The results are going to be checked twice in the UK first and then e-mailed to America for a final interpretation. We'll do it as quickly as we can, though."

I exhaled as I left the room and Joe stood up and hugged me. It was going to be hard going back to my cell without knowing the results, but I was confident there could only be one outcome.

Symbolic: Our home became a shrine of support (left) while family and friends take the campaign to an open top bus

Fight: Solicitor John Weate talks to the media about the High Court battle

Honour: The Kop mosaic demanding my freedom was a sight to behold

Wellwishers: More messages at Anfield as I spent my 21st birthday in prison

Ally: Mum and dad with Councillor Joe Anderson, one of my key campaigners

Decision: Jack Straw was granted the power to pardon me by the High Court, and (above) a badge of support

Defender: Jamie Carragher was always supportive of my fight for freedom

Heroes: Finally getting to meet Carra during a day release visit to Melwood and (left) Steven Gerrard warms up ahead of kick-off in one of our t-shirts

Magical: It was a privilege to be stood next to star striker Fernando Torres

Benitez: An amazing day was completed when I got to meet the gaffer

Show time: Stan Boardman helps mum and dad launch the benefit night outside the Empire Theatre and (right) the cast gather for the grand finale

Lobbying: My family join MEP Arlene McCarthy in taking the fight to No.10

Campaigners: Melissa, Laura, mum, and the Rt Rev James Jones

Rally: My parents and Cllr Anderson lead a protest march in the city in 2009

Home: In my bedroom (left) and (above) outside the Shankly Gates at Anfield

Return: It was a strange feeling being back in the city after so long away

"This will help us," said Joe. "I know it wasn't easy but it will be worth it."

Later that evening I was sat in my cell reading when a guard knocked on the door. "Get to the main office, Shields," he said. "There's a call for you." I was at the office in an instant and picked up the phone. It was Joe.

"You've passed with flying colours," he said. "The test shows you were telling the absolute truth throughout. Every one of your answers was 100%."

I smiled and clenched my fist in celebration. The test hadn't let me down. Surely the results would make people in the Government sit up and pay attention.

"They can't dismiss this," Joe said. "It's very rare for them to allow a prisoner to take a polygraph test. They've allowed you to take it and you've passed it."

Mr Cargill had explained that detectives in the USA rely on the results of polygraph tests and the latest test techniques are highly respected for their accuracy. Surely that had to mean something for my case.

I heard that Don Cargill went on Radio Merseyside to insist that even a so-called professional liar could not cheat the polygraph test.

I'm sure taking the test did help, but over a year-and-a-half later, I was still in jail.

UK OPENS NEW TALKS WITH BULGARIANS
AS SHIELDS SAILS THROUGH LIE TEST
Exclusive By Greg O'Keeffe & Ian Hernon

MICHAEL Shields today passed a lie detector test taken to help prove his innocence.

The world-renowned expert who carried out the test said the results proved Michael did not carry out the attack on waiter Martin Georgiev which led to his conviction for attempted murder in 2005.

British Polygraphers' Association examiner Don Cargill said the results also proved the 21-year-old was not even there when Mr Georgiev had a paving slab dropped on his head.

Today campaigners fighting to free Michael said they hoped the results would help persuade the British Government to pardon the Edge Hill student.

City Labour leader Joe Anderson, who was with Michael in Garth prison, Lancashire, said: "I'm absolutely thrilled that Michael has passed with flying colours.

"I never had a doubt that he wouldn't pass, but it is nevertheless a big boost for us. He got a 97.7 per cent result, which Don Cargill said was very high.

"Michael was nervous before the test because he has never done anything like this before, but he just answered the questions honestly, like he has always done.

"Mr Cargill was neutral before the test, but now he says he is convinced Michael is innocent and unfairly in prison.

"I hope Jack Straw will now see that we simply cannot let an innocent man be behind bars for any longer."

The jailed student was questioned for two hours and asked key questions relating to the attack on the Bulgarian waiter which led to his jailing in the Black Sea resort of Varna. The attack happened while Michael was in the resort following Liverpool FC's Champions League victory in Istanbul.

Now Cllr Anderson will bring the test results, along with other new evidence, to a meeting with justice secretary Jack Straw in January.

The Bishop of Liverpool, the Rt Rev James Jones, will also meet Mr Straw in London and ask him to pardon Michael.

Engineering student Michael is serving his 10-year sentence in a British jail after being convicted in Bulgaria of the attack in May 2005.

Home Office officials gave permission for the test to be carried out at the request of Michael's lawyers.

He was assessed by forensic psychologist Dr Keith Ashcroft before being connected to the polygraph computer.

Michael was asked if he was involved in the attack on Martin Georgiev and if he was in the area when it happened.

Mr Cargill has said results would be 95 to 98% accurate.

Michael's heart rate, blood pressure, sweat and breathing were monitored as he was questioned, and different readings were taken based on his responses.

Mr Cargill carries out tests for Channel Five's 'The Trisha Goddard Show'

Earlier this month the Echo revealed that a Liverpool man who saw the attack offered to go to Bulgaria and vouch for Michael.

Two men were also named in Parliament as potential witnesses but they later said they knew nothing that could free him.

Liverpool Riverside MP Louise Ellman used the protection of Parliamentary privilege to claim that witnesses named two men – Steven Clare and Graham Sankey – as the attackers.

– Liverpool Echo, December 21, 2007

POLYGRAPH EXPERT: SHIELDS IS TELLING US THE ABSOLUTE TRUTH
By Greg O'Keeffe

THE international expert who carried out Michael Shields' lie detector test today said the LFC fan "must be freed".

British Polygraphers' Association chairman Don Cargill said he was telling the "absolute truth" when he denied attacking waiter Martin Georgiev.

Mr Cargill, who has had talks with the Government about using his techniques in criminal cases, said justice minister Jack Straw should personally see the results of the test and pardon Michael.

Mr Cargill said: "In my professional opinion, Michael Shields did not assault Martin Georgiev, nor was he anywhere near the scene of the assault. Absolutely not.

"Beforehand I took a totally neutral view of this like I have to with every case.

"I now know that Michael is a genuine person who was telling the absolute truth.

"He is 100 per cent innocent and merely in the wrong part of the world at the wrong time. I only hope that the British Government can now let him out."

During the two-hour test, Mr Cargill asked Michael three major questions:

Q. Were you the person who hit Martin Georgiev on the head with a brick outside the Big Ben's restaurant on May 30, 2005?

A. No. Verdict: He was telling the truth.

Q. Were you involved in any way in the assault on Mr Georgiev before he was hit on the head with a brick?

A. No. Verdict: He was telling the truth.

Q. Were you at the scene of the assault on Mr Georgiev outside the Big Ben's restaurant?

A. No. Verdict: He was telling the truth.

Mr Cargill, also MD of the largest privately owned polygraph company in the UK, Nadac, added: "Michael came across as a nice young man. Remarkably, he was not angry or bitter despite the situation he has found himself in.

"I hope the results of the test are a boost for his parents and the people fighting to free him."

Michael's father, Michael Shields Snr, said: "Michael has wanted to take this test from day one. I'm made up he passed with flying colours."

City Labour leader Joe Anderson, who was with Michael in Garth prison, Preston, and who pushed for the test to take place said: "Michael volunteered to take this test because he wanted to clear his name. We pushed for it to take place and now we go forward and carry on the pressure to get him out."

The jailed student was asked dozens of other key questions relating to the attack on the Bulgarian waiter which led to his jailing in the Black Sea resort of Varna.

Michael was assessed by forensic psychologist Dr Keith Ashcroft before being connected to the polygraph computer.

Mr Cargill said results would be 95 to 98% accurate.

– Liverpool Echo, December 21, 2007

In the meantime, Arlene McCarthy was still hammering away at Europe for me. I was convinced she'd get nowhere because Bulgaria had said time and again they weren't interested in looking at the case. And I felt so let down by the European Court of Human Rights that I thought she was probably wasting her time.

The message had always been the same from Bulgaria – "We got the right man."

As far as I was concerned, it was only our Government and Jack Straw who could help me. It was the politicians who had promised my family they would do all they could.

It was the prime ministers who said they had sympathy for my case.

But even though I was convinced Bulgaria would never take a backwards step, we did get somewhere eventually. They admitted that all the new evidence which had come out couldn't be dismissed. But they could ignore it – and they were going to.

It was our problem.

YOU CAN FREE SHIELDS, BULGARIANS TELL BRITAIN
By Ben Schofield

MICHAEL Shields' campaign for freedom was bolstered last night after Bulgarian authorities said the UK Government does have the authority to pardon him.

Justice minister Jack Straw is exploring all avenues and taking legal advice to see if he can now intervene.

A letter from the justice minister in Sofia says Shields' fate effectively lies in British hands.

In it, Miglena Tacheva says there will be no further proceedings against Shields in Bulgaria and that his release from prison could therefore be "executed" by UK authorities.

Mrs Tacheva sent the note in response to a BBC investigation.

Shields' father yesterday pleaded with Mr Straw to release his son now the Bulgarians appear to have "wiped their hands of him".

Shields was convicted of attempted murder in Bulgaria following the Champions League final in Istanbul in 2005.

The 21-year-old is serving a 10-year sentence in Garth Prison, Lancashire.

He has maintained his innocence throughout and passed a lie detector test.

– Liverpool Daily Post, April 26, 2008

SHIELDS MAY BE INNOCENT – BULGARIANS
By Greg O'Keeffe

BULGARIAN politicians have admitted for the first time that new evidence casts doubt on Michael Shields' conviction.

The surprise revelation came from Bulgarian supreme judicial council member Tsoni Tsonev during a European Parliament hearing.

Mr Tsonev was speaking after Merseyside MEP Arlene McCarthy and Michael's lawyer Peter Weatherby tabled a petition claiming he was the victim of a legal miscarriage.

After the hearing in Strasbourg yesterday, the petitions committee voted to investigate the failure of the Bulgarian authorities to respond to the new dossier of evidence of witness statements which clear Michael, and lie detector tests which he passed.

But Bulgarian diplomats said they would not act regardless of what the European Parliament decided.

Mrs McCarthy and Mr Weatherby argued Bulgaria was breaching EU law by repeatedly refusing to agree a pardon or a retrial despite compelling evidence of the Reds fan's innocence.

The pair are part of a team who have tried to win the release of the Edge Hill 21-year-old convicted of hitting Bulgarian bartender Martin Georgiev with a paving stone after the 2005 European Cup final.

The Bulgarian Government has refused to reopen the case.

But president Georgi Parvanov has hinted he would not object to a UK pardon.

Justice minister Jack Straw is still waiting to hear from Queen's Counsel whether he could issue a pardon.

Mrs McCarthy said: "This is the first opportunity we have had to put the full facts on the table.

"We have taken this petition to the European Parliament because we are frustrated at the failure of the Bulgarian authorities to engage with Michael Shields' legal team.

"We have achieved this result with the support of other MEPs and in the face of continued resistance by the Bulgarians."

– Liverpool Echo, May 27, 2008

16. Home

While the fight to clear my name was constant, I had another goal to aim for in prison. I wanted to do everything possible to drop down the classification system.

If I kept my nose clean and followed all the rules, I knew I'd be down-graded, which in jail is a good thing.

A category C prison is more relaxed than a category B, and Haverigg was good for giving lads more opportunities to get involved in work. I knew that the next step after Haverigg was category D, and that would mean life would get a lot better.

Category D meant being allowed to leave prison for a day on temporary licence release. It also meant home visits.

In January 2009, I got a nice belated Christmas present. I was taken to one side and told I was being moved to Thorn Cross open prison in Warrington.

Not only was it an open jail, which meant it would be a lot more relaxed, it meant that I could taste freedom.

Initially it would be restricted to a day out in Warrington, but then there was the chance to go home.

Warrington is only 25 miles away from my house in Edge Hill, so visits would be a lot easier for my family. There would also be more Scousers in the prison, which was always a good thing.

Thorn Cross is a young offender institution built on the site of an old Navy air station.

I was getting used to packing up my things and moving prisons, so it wasn't a big deal leaving Haverigg. I was too excited about the possibility of getting out to worry about the change in routine.

The emphasis at Thorn Cross is on training and education. They're trying to prepare prisoners for the next step – the outside world. One of the first things they said was that there's opportunities to go to work outside of the prison.

I decided to throw myself into anything I could and make the best impression. It didn't take long for me to get some good news. While I was still adjusting to my new settings, I got notice of my first day release on a Saturday.

The night before, I got a bit nervous. What if something went wrong and it had to be cancelled in the morning? Was it going to feel really weird?

It had been a long time since I'd been outside a prison with any degree of personal freedom. Especially with my family allowed to be with me.

I was awake early and ready well before it was time. The screws led me to the gates of the prison and, after taking a deep breath, I walked out to see my mum and dad sitting waiting in the car.

The doors opened and Kelsey and Philip, my niece and nephew, came running towards me. They both jumped up and wrapped their arms and legs around me in a tag-team bear hug.

They didn't go far from my side for the whole day.

Mum and dad were beaming too and gave me big hugs when the kids agreed to let go for a minute. My sisters started fussing over me straight away.

It was a nice moment.

Then I got into the car and we made our plans. I had to be back by 4pm and the terms of the licence stipulated I had to stay in the Warrington area, so it didn't leave us with loads of options.

We decided to head to the local Golden Square shopping centre, and on the way we stopped at a McDonalds to grab some breakfast.

Before we left, the kids were fighting over who could sit by me in the car, so in the end I had to sit in the middle on the back seat with one either side.

My sisters were in another car. We were a real convoy as we drove through Warrington.

If I'm honest, it wasn't exactly what I'd dreamed my first proper meal outside of prison would be. I don't mind sausage and egg McMuffins, but I'd always longed for one of my mum's roasts or a slap-up meal.

But as I sat around the table with my family all eating our breakfast, it didn't matter what we were eating. The most important thing was we were together.

When we'd finished, we had a look around the shops. The first thing that hit me was how unusual it was being among ordinary people going about their weekend shopping.

I had some money on me and really wanted to do something normal like buy stuff from a shop. I took Kelsey and Philip into HMV and bought them each a DVD of their choice.

Then we decided to go bowling. I hadn't been since I was in my early teens and it brought back some nice memories of going with my mates.

The day was going quickly and after we'd finished bowling we went to a Nando's restaurant for some Portuguese food.

After we'd had our fill of chicken and rice, dad slipped some money into my hand and told me to settle-up. He knew I wanted to enjoy every bit of normality possible.

I'd been telling myself the day would fly by and knew it'd be sad when it was time to head back.

I tried to stay positive on the car journey back to Thorn Cross, telling myself it was only the beginning. Soon I'd be able to go home, even if I would always have to keep returning to a jail. Open or closed, category B or D, prison is still prison.

It was hard seeing everyone fighting off the tears as we said goodbye, and even harder watching them drive away.

It had been a great Saturday, but Saturday night was to be spent back in the prison routine. Not the plans of any other 22-year-old; getting on your smart clothes and heading into town for a few drinks while eyeing up the girls.

No, before long it would be back to my cell for a bit of TV before lights out. The only comfort was that we weren't locked in at Thorn Cross.

SHIELDS' MOVE TO OPEN JAIL
By Greg O'Keeffe

MICHAEL Shields is being moved to an open prison where he could be allowed home visits.

The 22-year-old earned a transfer to a Category D prison because of good behaviour while behind bars.

His family hope the move, possibly to an open prison in the north west, could happen before Christmas.

Category D prisoners can be released on licence to work in the community or go on "home leave".

The move came as Michael's mum Marie revealed she was going to Downing Street to present a personal letter to the prime minister's wife Sarah Brown.

Mrs Shields will be joined by other Liverpool mums including former Brookside and Royle Family actress Sue Johnston.

City Labour leader Joe Anderson, who has led the campaign to free him, said about the move to an open jail: "It's not before time.

"Michael should have been given this status and category a long time ago, of course he should not be in prison in the first place. He has been given no favours by the Government. Michael has earned the transfer by his exemplary behaviour. It speaks volumes for him."

Michael's solicitor John Weate, nominated legal aid solicitor of the year for his work for Michael, said: "This is wonderful news. Hopefully he will be moved within the next six weeks.

"The really positive thing is that this gives Michael the opportunity to go home at some point before his current release date in 2010."

Michael is currently in the category C prison at Haverigg in Cumbria. He has always denied being involved in the attack which happened after Liverpool FC's 2005 Champions League victory.

– Liverpool Echo, November 19, 2008

MICHAEL'S TASTE OF FREEDOM
AT BURGER BAR
By Greg O'Keeffe

MICHAEL Shields has enjoyed his first day of freedom on temporary release from jail.

The 22-year-old was allowed to spend Saturday with his family as a Government inquiry into his case continued.

Given day release from Thorn Cross prison in Warrington, he enjoyed a McDonald's meal and went bowling with his parents, sisters and other family members.

His father Michael Snr said he was telephoned by the prison on Friday night to say his son would be given temporary release on licence the next day, but only in Warrington.

He said: "It was a lovely day and we saw some joy in his face. We all went over in three cars and the kids were hanging off him all day. They were so happy and wouldn't leave him alone.

"The first thing we did was go to a McDonald's near the prison and have a coffee and something to eat. Then we went and had a look around the shops and Michael bought some DVDs for his niece and nephew from HMV.

"The kids were fighting over who could sit by him in the car. So in the end we had him in the middle on the back seat and one either side.

"After we'd looked around the shops we went to Nando's for our tea and Michael paid with some money we gave him.

"It was a special day and we enjoyed every moment. It was very emotional for us when we took him back to the prison and had to say bye. We can only hope now that Mr Straw comes to his senses and realises he can end the heartache for us."

The engineering student was jailed for 15 years for the attempted murder of Bulgarian barman Martin Georgiev after Liverpool's Champions League win in 2005, the sentence was later cut to 10 years on appeal.

He qualified for temporary day release shortly after being moved to the open jail, which holds 321 prisoners who each have a key to their single-room cells.

Last week, the Bishop of Liverpool, James Jones, wrote to justice minister Jack Straw to urge him to waste no time carrying out the inquiry into Michael's case, now entrusted to top QC, David Perry.

Mr Perry advised the Government not to bring charges against anyone in the cash for honours scandal.

He is also a deputy high court judge.
— Liverpool Echo, January 12, 2009

The time came for my first home leave. The ROTL (release on temporary licence) meant I was going back to Liverpool for the first time since my arrest.

It was a surreal experience. Mum and dad came to pick me up first thing in the morning and we made the short trip from Warrington back to Liverpool.

During the drive I was going through lot of different emotions. I'd been looking forward to going home for a long time. The thought had kept me going while I was sat in my dirty cell in Bulgaria especially.

But as we drove into Edge Hill, I couldn't shake a slight sadness that I wasn't coming home a free man.

I'd imagined that the first time I stepped into my house it would be with my name cleared, not with the thought that I'd be going back to prison after a day or two.

Still, I tried to look on the bright side. We drove into my street and the first thing that struck me was the yellow ribbons tied around the railings outside our house, then the massive poster with my face on saying 'Free Michael Shields'.

As I got out of the car and walked up the steps to our front door, I couldn't help remembering my mum waving me off in May 2005 as I jumped into my mate's waiting van full of excitement.

With dad's hand on my shoulder, I took a deep breath and walked through the front door. We went into the living room and sat down.

Nothing had really changed, but everything seemed smaller. The counsellor in prison had warned me to expect that, but it was a strange feeling.

As my mum put the kettle on and started to make breakfast, I ran upstairs to my room. It had been kept exactly the same, with my Liverpool posters still on the wall.

I lay on my bed for a couple of minutes staring at the ceiling trying to take everything in. Then my dad called up to me that breakfast was ready.

Sitting down alongside mum and dad, with everyone else buzzing around, and eating together was great. It was normal – or at least how normality should have been.

The rest of the weekend was a blur of visiting family and friends. Whenever it got a bit too much and I felt the pressure building up I'd go and sit quietly in my room.

It was something I'd feel regularly on home leaves. Because you've got such a limited amount of time to spend with your friends and family, it can all get a bit pressurised and claustrophobic.

That didn't stop me enjoying them though. Home leaves were my life-line and they got me used to the idea of being free again and getting back into my old life, even if it was just temporary.

Of course I also began to realise the size of the support I had in Liverpool. I read the Echo articles and listened to the radio phone-ins.

But the interesting thing was that even when I was walking around the city on my home leaves, hardly anyone recognised me.

I'd lost four stone since I was locked up. I was probably a bit taller and my face had changed.

Once I was walking around Liverpool city centre on a Saturday with my nephew Philip in his Liverpool kit.

Town was especially busy and we decided to walk along Lord Street and onto Church Street, teeming with shoppers. Not one person batted an eye-lid.

The worst thing about home leave was the last few hours before I had to go back. I began to get a feeling of dread in the pit of my stomach as the clock ticked down, and it got even worse when the time came to get into the car and head back to the prison.

The nice little glimpse of normality would be over and it'd be back to the boring humdrum of prison life away from my family.

MICHAEL RAN TO HIS ROOM . . .
HE HAD DREAMT OF IT FOR YEARS
Greg O'Keeffe

MICHAEL Shields has returned to his Liverpool home for the first time in three and a half years under new relaxed prison terms.

The 22-year-old was allowed to spend three days back with his family in Edge Hill, on temporary licence release from jail in Warrington.

Today his father Michael Snr described the emotional moment his son finally walked through the front door again since he left to watch Liverpool play in the Champion's League final in 2005.

And he told how the engineering student spent his first night back in his old bedroom after a poignant family meal.

But he insisted their ordeal is far from over, emphasising the agony of having to drive his son back to prison after the visit.

The 46-year-old window cleaner said: "It was incredibly emotional for us all but particularly his mum. She was waiting at the front door and saw him coming round the corner of our street in the car.

"She opened the door and put her arms around him as he walked in. Maria has been waiting for that moment a long time. We all have.

"He ran upstairs to his room and said he'd been dreaming of doing that for years. He was in control of his emotions and stood up like a man but everyone else was in tears.

"Maria did him an English breakfast when he came downstairs and he kept saying everything was really small in the house. I told him it was just because he hadn't been back for so long.

"He went on the laptop in the living room and was watching the Liverpool FC channel on TV. Then some of his friends came over and it was lovely to see him smiling and laughing with them. That first night he said he had a good sleep in his own bed.

"I was up early the next morning and went into his room to check on him and see if he was OK. It just felt normal for us all for the first time in ages. Then we had to take him back on the Friday afternoon and it was heart-breaking.

"After we dropped him back off at the jail we came home and sat in the empty house. Maria was crying and we just felt we shouldn't have had to do that. We were very low for that weekend knowing Jack Straw has the power to put an end to all this but hasn't.

"I feel like going and standing outside St George's Hall and asking why. Why Michael is still in prison. Why Jack Straw said he'd act quickly in reviewing Michael's case... Every day hurts us more."

Michael was given temporary release from a Wednesday morning to Friday afternoon last month. He is also allowed more frequent day-release where he must remain in Warrington.

His next three-day release period is due in March.

Mr Shields said: "When we were driving Michael home that first day, he couldn't believe how much the city had changed. We came to the top of Everton valley and he was amazed by the skyline with the wind turbines and the new Beetham tower. I think it was very strange for him."

Today, Conservative MP and shadow home secretary Chris Grayling will visit the Shields family home to lend his support to their campaign to get a Royal Pardon for Michael.

The MP for Epsom and Ewell has written to Jack Straw asking why the review into Michael's case has taken so long and will ask the family what extra support he can provide in person.

Mr Grayling is also the Tory shadow minister responsible for Merseyside, a reprisal of the role Michael Heseltine carried out during the previous Conservative Government.

City Labour leader Joe Anderson said he has written to Jack Straw telling of his "shame" that a Labour Government is keeping "an innocent man" in jail.

He said: "We are entering the ninth week since the judgement was given that Jack Straw has the power to release Michael Shields.

"As a legal man himself, the Secretary of State for Justice must understand that the evidence we have provided him with casts serious doubts on the safety of the conviction.

"He has already asked David Perry QC to look into the evidence and we can only hope he will come to the same conclusion.

"As a senior member of the Labour party and the leader of that party in my own city, I am ashamed that this Government is keeping an innocent man behind bars.

"This Government should be less interested in the technicalities of legal arguments and more interested in no longer perpetuating a grave miscarriage of justice.

"Mr Straw has said he is reluctant to interfere in the legal *process in Michael's case, but he rightly intervened in the case of Jade Goody and Jack Tweed, proving he has discretionary power to intervene on humanitarian grounds."*

– Liverpool Echo, February 25, 2009

17. The Final Straw

Jack Straw had a habit of crushing our hopes whenever we thought there was light at the end of the tunnel.

My lawyers were convinced that regardless of what Bulgaria said, our own Government had the key to release me. We felt the power was in Jack Straw's hands. It turned out he felt differently.

In yet another setback he wrote to John Weate saying there was nothing we could do. It was a blow, but John and Peter decided to take him to High Court.

It seemed mad taking our own Justice Secretary to court but they were convinced he was wrong. I just had to hope they were right.

STRAW: IT'S OUT OF MY HANDS
By Marc Waddington

JUSTICE minister Jack Straw has told the family of Michael Shields he has no power to pardon the jailed Reds fan.

The 22-year-old's chances of freedom now rest on whether High Court judges review the decision and decide the government can end his 10-year sentence early.

Yesterday, a letter from Mr Straw to Michael's lawyer John Weate explained the power to release the Reds' fan lay in Bulgaria, where he was jailed in 2005, not Westminster.

Michael is now serving a reduced 10-year sentence at Haverigg prison, in Cumbria, after being moved to the UK in 2006.

Mr Weate said: "Mr Straw has basically said under the treaty

*provided for the transfer, the authority to deal with the issue is
vested in the country where sentence was passed, not the
receiving country.*

*"A judge will now have to either grant permission for a
judicial review to decide whether the jurisdiction exists, or
refuse, in which case we will have to re-apply.*

*"But the fight will go on and we believe when we go to court,
the case is strong enough to say Straw does have jurisdiction."*

*Michael's father, Michael Shields senior, said: "Jack Straw
does not seem to have changed his position much, and did not
say he had anything against a judicial review.*

*"So why did they leave it to the very last minute to get in touch
with us?*

*"If he had responded earlier, such as when he came to
Liverpool three weeks ago, then Michael could be 21 days
closer to freedom."*

– Liverpool Echo, September 24, 2009

As ever, while my lawyers were fighting Jack Straw's decision that he
was not legally entitled to grant me a pardon, all I could do was wait.

I couldn't get too excited on the day of the High Court case
because I felt so far removed from it all the way back up North in
Thorn Cross. The day itself almost felt irrelevant.

I was working as an assistant in the prison gym at the time. It was
a good job which involved maintaining all the equipment, cleaning
the gym every morning and making sure everything was in its right
place. But it also meant I was able to use the equipment whenever
it was quiet and I loved it. If there was a sport class on I could
usually latch onto that, too. The hours were 8.30am to 11.30am and
then 1pm to 4.30pm.

The senior officer who ran the gym said I could take the day of the
High Court case off and I reluctantly agreed. I shouldn't have
bothered. Instead of being occupied and having something to keep

my mind off the outcome, I just sat in my cell and fretted.

That night, Peter Weatherby phoned me to say it had gone well but, you guessed it, I was going to have to wait for the decision. The three judges needed time to go through the evidence which had been put before them and make up their mind.

Time dragged on and I waited. It wasn't like I wasn't used to it.

About a month later, I was taken into the office and was told the judges had made their minds up. It was the best news I could have hoped for. The judges had said Straw could pardon me and even added that the ID parade in Bulgaria had been unfair. That was an understatement, but it felt great to have their backing.

Peter wisely told me not to get too carried away.

"When the media finds out it might look like you'll be out within days, but it's very unlikely to happen like that. Don't get carried away," he said.

"If people start telling you to pack your bags, then blank it out. It won't happen like that unfortunately."

SHIELDS WINS BATTLE
IN LEGAL PARDON BID
By Greg O'Keeffe

JAILED Liverpool fan Michael Shields won an important High Court battle today in his bid for a free pardon.

Two senior judges ruled that Justice Secretary Jack Straw did have the "power and jurisdiction" to exercise the ancient "royal prerogative of mercy" in the case of Shields, who was convicted abroad but transferred to a UK prison to finish his sentence.

But the judges also ruled that it was for Mr Straw alone – and not the courts – to decide how to exercise that power.

The ruling means Shields does not have an automatic right to his freedom.

Shields, now 22, is serving 10 years for the attempted murder of a barman at the Big Ben diner in Varna, Bulgaria, in 2005.

MPs, clergymen, Liverpool FC players and many others have backed the call to free him on the basis that he is innocent.

Mr Straw's legal team argued at a recent High Court hearing in London that there was no jurisdiction to grant Shields a free pardon.

They warned that, if the Justice Secretary did intervene, the move could be seen as criticism of the foreign court that found Shields guilty.

But Justice May and Mr Justice Maddison, sitting in London, said: "We declare that he does have such power and jurisdiction."

The judges stressed that it was not for the court to say "whether or how that power may be exercised".

The judges ruled the Justice Secretary did have power under Article 12 of the Convention on the Transfer of Sentenced Persons 1983 "to consider at least granting pardon to Michael Shields on the facts presented to this court."

— Liverpool Echo, December 17, 2008

Even though I knew he was talking sense, I started to believe a bit. Then we got Straw's reply and it meant more waiting.

Straw was going to ask Merseyside Police to hold an inquiry and open up the case. OK there was going to be no quick fix, but it was great that the case was going to be properly investigated.

The police weren't able to re-interview me, but they were allowed to speak to the man known as Witness A who saw the attack, and they tried to speak to Sankey, Wilson and Thompson.

I later heard the police took a long and detailed statement from Witness A, and I hoped Sankey and the others would finally tell the full truth.

I didn't know it at the time, but the police report was good for me. They agreed that the ID evidence used to convict me would never have been accepted in a British court. In our country it wouldn't even get to trial if somebody under arrest for an offence was pictured in a newspaper before they were even charged. The trial could never be considered fair.

I also learnt later that Sankey, Wilson and Thompson had refused to be interviewed. It was so frustrating. More than four years on and none of them had developed a conscience. You'd think the little voice in the back of their heads would have been getting louder but somehow they were ignoring it.

Ultimately, I wasn't surprised they had ignored the police though. It made me angry, but I just couldn't allow it to build up inside me. I didn't want it to bubble up and erupt. It was no good to me holding onto the anger.

Meanwhile, I managed to get into a bit of bother. I'd had a mobile phone while I was in Haverigg and then in Thorn Cross too. It's illegal, but it's fairly common.

Prisoners would normally use their phones quietly at night time in their cells. I was still speaking to my dad on the prison phone for five minutes every day just to keep things looking normal.

But when we'd gone through the motions of speaking over the phone out on the corridor, I'd go back to my cell, shut the door, and call him on my mobile. Then we could talk properly and more relaxed. I was on it almost every night.

I'd have to listen out for the sounds of footsteps of a guard just in case. Getting caught would probably have meant being moved to another closed prison and getting days added onto my sentence.

I'd bought my phone from another prisoner a few weeks after I arrived. The problem was that there was an officer tasked with keeping his eye on prisoners who may have had phones or been up to no good. The security governor, as we called him, kept a file. We called it the 'gossip file'. Only he could see it because the data was protected. No other guards could look at it, but the last thing I wanted was to be added to it.

Then, one day, I was on home leave and I was speaking to my friend back in Thorn Cross using the social networking site Facebook on our phones.

My friend had been busted with his phone. They hauled him in and while they were checking his phone, they found our Facebook messages. Technically I was OK because I'd been out on leave and there's no law on using a phone outside.

But I was still grilled about it by the security governor and it was an edgy time. They seemed very suspicious that I had a phone and I knew I couldn't afford to get caught.

They were annoyed that I knew he had a phone and hadn't told them. As if I was going to tell them though. I was certainly more wary after that.

Yes, I had a phone and if I'd been caught I would have had to have held my hands up, but it would've been bad.

Shortly after the situation with the mobile phone, I left my job in the gym for a while. I was on edge constantly waiting for Jack Straw's decision and I'd started to show it.

Sometimes if a guard told me what to do, I'd tell them to shut up or refuse. I knew I shouldn't speak to them like that but I was so frustrated. The constant rules and regulations were getting me down.

I asked to be moved from the gym and they transferred me to the catering division. It wasn't that I disliked anyone in the gym, but I needed a change. After a few weeks doing that I was desperate to get back in the gym. Luckily the gym officer was a good fella and he allowed me to come back.

Christmas came and went with the same depressing routine and sadness. Then, in January, 2009 I got some great news.

Liverpool FC had invited me to visit their Melwood training ground on my next home leave. I couldn't wait.

It was all set for a Friday, which was the last day of my three-day home leave. I went up with my parents, Nicky Allt and Franny Banner. It was just after the team had their breakfast while they were getting ready for training. I was sitting in a side room and one by one the players popped in to say hello. First it was Ryan Babel, then Pepe Reina and Xabi Alonso, then the coach Gary Ablett came in, Sammy Lee, Dirk Kuyt and then Carragher. Jamie spoke to us for ages. He really is just one of the boys. A normal down to earth lad. I'll always be grateful for the way he in particular spoke up for me.

Unfortunately, Steven Gerrard wasn't there because he was in court, but I've got to admit we did have a giggle. There I was on home leave from prison and our captain was in court.

The manager Rafa Benitez was the biggest surprise. He often looks very intense and serious on the TV, but he was very relaxed and had a dry sense of humour. He had us laughing with stories about his visits to Arrowe Park hospital with kidney stones. Then he was telling us all about how he thought Alex Ferguson had too much power and influence with the FA. It was a few weeks before he hit out about it in front of the TV cameras when he listed his 'facts'. I'd had a sneak preview. It must have been winding him up for months.

He was very generous with his time and it was a special day. The end of home leaves are normally horrible.

You sink lower in the car seat and into misery as you approach the gates, but this time I went back with a spring in my step and loads of stories for the lads.

It was to be the last really happy memory before one of my lowest ever moments in July. All the rumours were that we were going to finally get a positive decision from Jack Straw. In the back of my mind I tried to stay cautious but I couldn't ignore the people saying my time had finally come.

Then I was called into an office again and one of the governors sat me down.

"I'm afraid it's bad news," he said, "although it's not final."

He went on to read me a prepared statement given to him by the justice office which outlined why Jack Straw was provisionally refusing to pardon me.

STRAW REJECTS SHIELDS PARDON
– MOTHER COLLAPSES AS JACK STRAW REJECTS PARDON FOR LFC FAN
By John Fahey

JUSTICE Secretary Jack Straw last night said he understood the "strong emotions" felt by the family of Michael Shields, after refusing him a pardon due to the "rule of law".

Shields, of Edge Hill, was jailed for 15 years in Bulgaria, in 2005, for the attempted murder of a barman following Liverpool FC's Champions League triumph in Turkey.

His mother, Maria Shields, collapsed after hearing the news and later described Mr Straw's decision as "like a knife in the back."

Mr Straw stressed his decision – in which he concluded he was unable to decide whether the 22-year-old was "morally and technically innocent" – was provisional.

"I understand, of course, the strong emotions felt by the Shields family and his many supporters in Liverpool and way beyond Liverpool," said Mr Straw. "What I ask people in return is that you have to operate in this country by the rule of law."

Mr Straw, speaking at the Ministry of Justice in London, said he would be prepared to meet the Shields family and said his legal team now had a month to put forward more evidence.

"Of course, I am open to further representations from Mr Shields and I am seeking them," he said.

Father, Michael senior, said: "We are absolutely devastated by today's announcement from Jack Straw.

"After four years of tireless campaigning, we had every hope and belief that Michael was about to be pardoned for a crime he did not commit. I have spoken to Michael and he is absolutely distraught.

"We have been led a merry dance by the Government.

"We have been kept completely in the dark and still have no idea what is happening.

"Michael received an email in prison today telling him his

pardon had been refused, but he does not know the reason why. I don't know how much more we can take as a family.

"One minute we are expecting him to be pardoned and released, then the next minute all our hopes are dashed.

"All I can say is that Michael, his family and all the campaigners are absolutely heartbroken today."

Mr Shields's mother, Maria, said: "I just can't believe it – it's a disgrace".

Family solicitor John Weate vowed to fight on.

"To get a pardon, you have to get a higher degree of certainty, and I think that's what they're talking about.

"If we've got a further 28 days to make representations, then we will definitely do that.

"I have been in this line of work for 37 years and this lad is as innocent as you and me."

Labour leader Cllr Joe Anderson said the decision left him "ashamed to be a member of the Labour Party".

– Liverpool Daily Post, July 3, 2009

"He has given you 28 days to make any last representations though," continued the governor.

It didn't matter now, I told myself. It was over. He'd killed me off. There was no way back.

"We will get the chaplain to come and talk to you," said the governor as he handed me the huge pile of papers which was Straw's decision in full. As I flicked through it, my heart sank lower and lower.

They gave me a phone to tell my family. I phoned John Weate my solicitor and he didn't even know. He was cursing down the phone and I asked for my dad's mobile number. Eventually I got hold of my dad and I ended up trying to pick him up. I could hear my mum wailing in the background.

The chaplain came in. 'Don't make it worse – nobody has died', I thought. This was going to get me down even more.

We had a quick chat and he expressed his sadness on my behalf. I told him politely that I wanted to be alone to get my head around the paperwork.

I plodded back to my cell and sat there numb, reading through it. One of my mates from a cell just around the corner came in. I felt sorry for him because I'd always chew his ear off when I was in a bad mood about the case.

"Here have a look," I said, handing him the dossier. He flicked through it for a few minutes.

"There's nothing I can say to you," he said.

That was it. It was all about waiting until May 2010 when my sentence was over anyway. All hope was gone then.

At least I can just get my head down now and do my sentence like a prisoner, I thought. No more court cases or lie detectors. No more constant ups and downs. I just had to last almost another year. Time went very slowly. I wrote lots of angry ranting letters to my pen pals. The anger threatened to get the better of me. I preferred it if nobody asked me about the case or Jack Straw because if they did they regretted it because there would be a 10 minute rant.

I knew Peter and John hadn't given up and were staying positive, but all I was focused on was next May.

SHIELDS' TEAM ATTACK STRAW
By Greg O'Keeffe

JACK Straw was today accused of breaking his word to Michael Shields ahead of a final decision on whether to pardon him.

It came as the Justice Secretary's initial reason for refusing to pardon the 22-year-old is blasted in a 26-page last-ditch report by his legal team.

Speaking ahead of the final Government decision, expected next month, city Labour leader Joe Anderson said: "Jack Straw has said many times to various people that he will do all he *can to assist Michael's case.*

"But his own report into why he is considering refusal seems to show he has done exactly the opposite.

"He has broken his word. All of the evidence would lead most reasonable, fair-minded people to the conclusion that there has to be significant doubt about the safety of Michael's conviction.

"But instead Jack Straw misinterpreted the High Court's ruling and even ignored a vital part of what they said. It's scandalous."

The document prepared by the Liverpool FC supporter's lawyers sets out a series of arguments against Jack Straw's decision earlier this month.

– Liverpool Echo, July 20, 2009

18. Free At Last

The only goal left to me was to finish my sentence and make the best use of my time with college courses and working in the gym.

Even up until that last day in Thorn Cross I didn't let myself believe there was any hope.

I knew that mum and dad were going to meet Jack Straw in Blackburn at the end of August. They seemed positive afterwards and said it had gone well, but I was having none of it.

Of course he'd be nice to them and say the right things. He'd shake their hands and say he knew what they were going through like he had in the past. But then he'd just turn around and listen to his advisors telling him to let me rot.

September 9, 2009 started like any other day.

I was in the gym wearing rubber gloves with a mop in my hands cleaning up. Two guards walked over to me.

"One of the governors needs to talk to you about your Prince's Trust course in January," said one. But something didn't seem right. Why did they want to talk about it now? It wasn't for ages. I got a sick feeling. They were obviously taking me to one side to tell me it was bad news. They'd got Jack Straw's final decision.

I followed them into the office where the top governor was waiting. She's the number one in the prison. It must be something big, I thought.

As I walked through the corridors with two prisoners either side, some of my mates saw me.

"Are you alright? What's happening?" one asked. You don't see prisoners heading to the Number One's office every day.

"It's OK. I'll be back in five minutes," I said.

Then I stepped into her office. I was barely past the door when she turned around smiling.

"You're an innocent man," she said. "You're free."

I sat down and started shaking. I probably went white. I'd dreamt about this moment many times and I actually did pinch my arm just to check if I was still dreaming.

"I've had a fax from the justice department," she added. "It's saying we should let you go as soon as possible."

I tried to phone home and couldn't get through. The number was engaged. Again I got hold of John Weate first and he was shouting down the phone in delight. Then my mum answered the house phone crying.

"Forget about all that," I joked. "I need picking up now."

I still couldn't get my head around it. When were they going to turn around and say that it had all been a big mistake?

"I need to get my things," I mumbled.

They led me back to my cell with the governor in tow.

"I can't leave your side," she said. "You're not a prisoner now, you're a free man. I can't let you wander about on your own."

"What's going on?" said one of my mates as we walked past.

I started to laugh. "I'm out," I managed to say. "They've given me the pardon."

It was happening so quickly. I managed to shout goodbye to some of the lads who were around but there were others at work that I never got the chance to say my farewells to.

I started to prise my postcards off the wall. They were stuck on using coffee whitener and water – better known as prison glue. I carefully prised off the signed pictures of Steven Gerrard and Jamie Carragher. Then all my post cards from wellwishers throughout the world.

"I want to leave my Playstation and my radio for the lads," I said.

"You've got to take it, it's yours," said the governor.

"I'll just leave it to the prison and you can give it to the lads. My bag is breaking my back anyway with all the documents inside."

I didn't have time to pick up my mug and toiletries. My ID card was still in my prison-issue jeans which were in the gym. I wanted to keep it but didn't want to linger another moment.

Back to the office we went and I was handed my normal clothes to change into as I waited for my lift.

The senior officer of the gym came in and shook my hand.

"Well done," he said. "I'm made-up for you. You deserve it."

Slowly it started to sink in a bit. I was going home.

"Do you want water?" they asked.

"Yeah."

"Do you want tea?"

"Yeah."

"Which do you want? Both?" he asked laughing.

I wasn't even listening properly.

"Come and have a look at this," said the senior gym officer, as he pointed out of the office window at all the press photographers and journalists outside.

"Don't worry, they're not for you," he smiled. "It's just a load of bird watchers."

I was waiting for half an hour. It might not seem like a long time, but it was to me. It was the longest half an hour ever.

Eventually I saw Joe Anderson's car roll into the prison gates, drive up the main path and pull up by the side entrance.

I was led down to meet them and saw my mum and dad jump out and run towards me. They threw their arms around me, both crying.

The governor led us inside to the office. "I'll give you a minute," she said.

As soon as she shut the door I looked at my mum.

"Come on let's go," I said. "I don't want to spend another minute in here. Just take me home."

My dad picked up my bag and led me outside to the flashing cameras and shouted questions.

I got into the car and as we pulled away the amount of press shocked me. They were lined up shouting and waving to get my attention. I hadn't had time to have a wash or a shave and looked rough.

"I'll slow down and you can give them a smile and a thumbs up," said Joe. Really I just wanted him to put his foot down, but I smiled.

As we drove out of the prison gates, I didn't look back.

Joe explained we were going to the Echo offices in Liverpool city centre for a press conference. Everything still felt like a blur. It was a happy blur though. We took a slight detour before we went to the Echo. I was desperate for a shave and a change of clothes. Thankfully mum and dad had brought me some. We went to Joe's house and I had a shower and got rid of the stubble. I slipped into my combats and trainers. Pulled on my own T-shirt instead of the boring prison issue outfit.

It felt good. As soon as I was ready I walked into the living room. My sisters Melissa and Laura had arrived while I'd been in the shower. Everyone was glued to the BBC and Sky footage of my case. On the TV screen was the picture of me walking out of the prison with mum and dad only an hour earlier. Surreal wasn't the word. Every time the presenter said 'Michael Shields' my stomach flipped. I'll never get used to it.

The press conference went better than I thought. I sat alongside Joe, Louise Ellman, John, Peter, Arlene McCarthy and the Bishop of Liverpool. The people handling the conference had asked me if I had any objection to the Bishop reading a statement on my behalf. I didn't – if anything it was a relief. I wasn't getting off that easily though, the last words were saved for me. When it was my turn I stood up, took a deep breath, and tried to read it clearly and slowly.

"Thanks to my supporters, I never walked alone," I said.

Every time I smiled or laughed during the 45 minutes the cameras went mad. I must seem like a miserable bugger the rest of the time, I thought. Later that evening I went to a posh hotel in Cheshire with my family and friends.

My head had almost stopped spinning. Almost. Dad handed me my first pint as a free man. It tasted pretty good. We ordered food and watched Steven Gerrard score twice for England as they qualified for the World Cup.

Stevie was on fire, the drinks flowed. Nobody stopped smiling all night. The form Liverpool are in we could win the league I thought. Now I'll be able to go back to the Kop. My dad kept my season ticket open for me. He never stopped believing this day would come. None of them did.

SHIELDS FREED AFTER STRAW PARDONS LIVERPOOL FC FAN
Exclusive by Greg O'Keeffe

MICHAEL Shields was today set to be freed from jail after he was finally pardoned by Justice Secretary Jack Straw.

The 22-year-old has won his four-and-a-half-year fight to clear his name after a dramatic Government U-turn on his case.

In July, Mr Straw ruled he was not convinced the Edge Hill student was "morally and technically" innocent of the attempted murder of a Bulgarian waiter in 2005.

But today he announced that new evidence has convinced him to release Michael.

Campaigners who have fought for his release were gathering at the Shields family home in Edge Hill to celebrate with mother Maria and father Michael Snr.

It comes after Mr Straw held last-ditch talks with Michael's parents and City Labour leader Joe Anderson at his constituency office in Blackburn on August 28.

The Echo understands new evidence presented to the Secretary of State for Justice at the meeting has led to his re-think.

Mr Straw has also come under increasing pressure from Merseyside MPs and crucially from Britain's leading unions.

TUC leader, Southport-born Brendan Barber, also wrote an open letter to Mr Straw calling for him to free Michael, and labelling the case a "shocking miscarriage of justice".

Cllr Anderson said: "This is the news we have all been waiting so long for. At last an innocent man is being freed from prison for a crime he did not commit. It hasn't come a moment too soon but we're delighted."

– Liverpool Echo, September 9, 2009

SHIELDS: TODAY IS THE FIRST DAY
OF THE REST OF MY LIFE
By Greg O'Keeffe

MICHAEL Shields was today starting his new life as a free man back in his Liverpool home.

The 22-year-old Liverpool fan was trying to re-adjust to normality after a whirlwind 24 hours which saw him finally granted a royal pardon by justice secretary Jack Straw.

He emerged smiling from prison in Warrington yesterday morning and was driven to face the world's media at a press conference in the Echo's city centre offices.

He thanked his tireless supporters and declared: "Today is the first day of the rest of my life."

The engineering student's release means he is "technically and morally innocent" of the attempted murder of waiter Martin Georgiev in Bulgaria following the Reds' 2005 European Cup win. He was sentenced to 15 years but the term was later reduced to 10 years.

Michael spent last night enjoying a meal and low-key celebration with his mother Maria, father Michael Snr, and sisters Melissa and Laura. He now plans to attend Liverpool's match against Burnley at Anfield on Saturday as a guest of the club. It will be the season-ticket holder's first game since 2005's UEFA Champions League final in Istanbul.

During yesterday's conference, wearing a black LFC T-shirt, he praised his supporters, saying: "I would like to say a massive thank you to all those people out there – including Liverpool and Everton football fans – who have supported me and my family over the last four years by writing letters, by protesting, by marching. Your voices were heard. Thanks to you, I knew I would never walk alone."

Michael was stunned when he first faced the media but maintained his composure throughout the conference.

The Bishop of Liverpool, the Rt Rev James Jones, read a statement on his behalf. It said: "The last four years have been the hardest four years of my life.

"They have been a living hell.

"Today is the first day of the rest of my life.

"And I am only sitting here today thanks to the love, support and tireless campaigning of a number of people, some of whom are here today.

"In particular, I want to take this opportunity to say a public thank you to Councillor Joe Anderson, who led this campaign.

"I'd also like to thank Louise Ellman MP, Arlene McCarthy MEP, Bishop James Jones and my legal team, John Weate and Peter Weatherby.

"All have been so solid in their support for me and my family.

"Most of all I want to thank my mum and dad, my sisters, my family and my friends, who never for one minute doubted my innocence and who stood by me every step of the way.

"I couldn't have made it without their love.

"It's a hard thing to be locked away for a crime you did not commit.

"I was just 18 when I was arrested.

"I'm now 22 and face having to rebuild my life which was shattered by the failure of two legal systems, one here in the UK and one in Bulgaria.

"Today is a happy day for me but one of mixed emotions too.

"I am a free man, yes, but it should not have come to this.

"I now face a hard battle to adjust to normality.

"To find a job. To resume friendships. To build an ordinary life.

"I would like to extend my sympathy to the familly of Martin Georgiev, who was the innocent victim of an unprovoked attack.

"He and his family, like me and mine, have been denied justice for four long years.

"My priority now is to spend time with my loved ones. To slowly begin to plan for a future as an innocent man."

He was told by the governor of Thorn Cross Young Offenders' Institution in Warrington shortly after 9am yesterday that he would be released. His parents had received a phone call from Mr Straw shortly beforehand.

Dad Michael Shields snr, a window cleaner, was up a ladder in Childwall at the time. He said: "It was a very emotional phone call which came directly from Jack Straw.

"We just thanked him for all the work he has put in.

"It's such a special day, we are so pleased to have him back with us."

According to Shields' solicitor John Weate and barrister Peter Weatherby, the justice secretary took the decision after receiving new "corroborative" evidence during a meeting with the family at the end of August.

The evidence was that members of Shields' family went to visit Graham Sankey at his Liverpool home where he admitted committing the crime Shields was jailed for.

Apparently, Mr Straw did not know about this despite knowing Sankey had also provided a written confession to the attack, which he later retracted.

Now, the legal team hope the Bulgarian authorities reopen the case after considering the pardon and a Merseyside Police report concluding there were huge doubts over the case against Shields.

Liverpool councillor Joe Anderson, who led the freedom

campaign, said: "I am just delighted he is out.

"He deserves to be.

"I have known this man for four-and-a-half years and he is like a son to me.

"I know full well he was innocent and I have seen him grow into a mature young man who is not bitter."

There was no answer at the family home of Graham Sankey yesterday.

Previous legal representatives of Mr Sankey declined to comment.

– Liverpool Echo, September 9, 2009

MICHAEL SHIELDS PARDON WELCOMED BY LIVERPOOL POLITICAL AND RELIGIOUS LEADERS
By Marc Waddington

POLITICAL and religious leaders have spoken of their joy at the release of Michael Shields.

City council leader Cllr Warren Bradley and Labour Riverside MP Louise Ellman were amongst the first to speak of their delight at the news.

Cllr Bradley said his release after a lengthy campaign to free him was a "victory for common sense".

He added: "I welcome the decision of the justice secretary to grant Michael Shields a pardon and facilitate his release from prison.

"Michael must now receive the appropriate support which will enable him to begin to rebuild his life following the nightmare situation he needlessly found himself in. I will work alongside opposition leader Cllr Joe Anderson to assist him in finding new opportunities."

Labour Riverside MP Louise Ellman added: "I am overjoyed at Jack Straw's decision.

"Michael has suffered a gross miscarriage of justice, incarcerated for four years for a crime he did not commit and for which another man has confessed.

"I pay tribute to Michael's family and the people of Liverpool *for their remarkable courage and persistence."*

North West Euro MP Arlene McCarthy added: "Finally after over four years of fighting and numerous setbacks Michael is free.

"It is fantastic news and I now hope that Michael can start to rebuild his life.

"The Bulgarian authorities' failure to accept their democratic responsibilities to right a terrible wrong has meant that we have been left with no option but to put pressure on our own Government and on Jack Straw personally to do the right thing and free Michael."

And the Bishop of Liverpool, the Rev James Jones, added that he "had always believed in Michael's innocence."

He added: "I am so happy for him. I saw him a few weeks ago and was impressed by how he has coped.

"He and his family have been through a terrible ordeal. I hold them in my prayers as they rebuild their lives."

CLUB WELCOMES STRAW DECISION

LIVERPOOL Football Club today welcomed the news that Michael Shields has been pardoned by the Justice Secretary Jack Straw. The 22-year old Liverpool supporter was sentenced to ten years in prison in Bulgaria for an attack on a barman in 2005, but he has always maintained his innocence and supporters have campaigned tirelessly to clear his name.

Today's announcement, clearing Michael of any involvement in the attack, meant those efforts have not been in vain and Liverpool Football Club was today delighted to hear the news.

A club statement said: "It's great news that Michael has been granted a pardon by the justice secretary Jack Straw.

"We know how difficult the last four years have been for Michael and his family and everyone at the club, the staff, the players and the fans have tried to support them during this time. We hope now that Michael and his family will be able to move on with their lives and look to the future."

– Liverpool Echo, September 9, 2009

STEVEN GERRARD: MICHAEL SHIELDS INSPIRED MY ENGLAND PERFORMANCE
By Dominic King

STEVEN GERRARD today reflected on one of his most satisfying nights in an England shirt – after revealing he took inspiration for his heroics from Michael Shields.

Liverpool skipper Gerrard scored twice last night as England thrashed Croatia 5-1 at Wembley to book their place at next summer's World Cup finals in style.

Those headers took Gerrard's international tally to 16 in 76 appearances and he clearly took great contentment from the standing ovation he was given when substituted late on.

But the in-form midfielder admitted he was just as pleased by the news earlier in the day that Shields' horrific four-year ordeal had been ended with a royal pardon.

"It's fantastic news both for Michael and his family," said Gerrard, who returned to Melwood today to start preparations for Saturday's clash with Burnley.

"I'm really pleased for all of them. It was a good day for me, scoring two goals and qualifying for the World Cup having switched on the television earlier in the day and seeing the news about Michael. It gave me a real boost."

Meanwhile, Michael Shields and his family have been invited by the Reds to be guests at Saturday's game against Burnley.

– Liverpool Echo, September 10, 2009

The Future

I don't know what the future holds for me now. I've missed out on so much. I want to get back to normality. To make plans for the future like anyone else.

I want to enjoy the luxury of saying to my mates: "Let's go to this concert in a few weeks." To be able to relax and not live my life in the outside world like time is on a meter and every second counts. Without the pressure of home leaves.

At the same time I've got to readjust. In prison when things are getting on top of you, it's easy to shut your cell door and go into a world of your own. That's not always possible in the real world.

I want to get a job and work nine to five. University isn't for me; I've had enough of institutions.

I don't want this case to mark me for life. I'd like for it all to be forgotten about one day. I hope people don't come up to me in 10 years and say: "Weren't you that kid who was locked up in Bulgaria?"

I'll never get used to seeing my face on TV or hearing my name mentioned. It always embarrasses me. I always get that feeling in the pit of my stomach.

The experience has changed me. I'm more streetwise, I'm more political and I appreciate the smaller things in life more. Playing footy with my nephew or looking around my city at the buildings, new and old.

During my penultimate home release before the final decision I went up to Everton Brow and gazed out over the city. The skyline had changed so much. I didn't recognise the Beetham West Tower and my old school had already been demolished. As the wind whipped around me, it was a bittersweet moment.

I'd love to go back to anonymity straight away, but at the same time I want my story to be told. It's important that people realise that what happened to me could happen again. It's important to me that people learn some lessons. I want something positive to come from this.

The future is wide open. It's scary but it's brilliant.

Michael Shields

Thank You

Michael Shields would like to thank the following people:

First and foremost my mum and dad for their endless love and support, my sisters Melissa and Laura and their partners, my nephew Philip and niece Kelsey, my Nan, Joe Anderson, his wife Margaret and all their family, my lawyers Peter Weatherby and John Weate, Louise Ellman, Arlene McCarthy, the Bishop of Liverpool James Jones, former Lord Mayor of Liverpool Steve Rotheram and wife Sandra, the Hillsborough Justice Campaign, the Spirit of Shankly union, Gerry White (Rest in Peace), Fair Trials International, Derek Lee and the Parkmore Group, Paul and Julian Flannagan, their families and the Flannagan Group, Brendan Barber and the TUC, Bob Croxton, the Shields and Graney families, the Liverpool Echo, the Daily Mirror, Brian Reade, Radio City, Kevin Sampson, Tony Barrett, Nicky Allt, Dave Kirby, all the taxi drivers of Liverpool, Liverpool FC and its fans, Everton FC and its fans, Jamie Carragher, Steven Gerrard, the Liverpool Labour Party, Malcolm Feld, Gina Feld, Izzy Feld, Lyn Staunton, Gloria Gaynor, Atomic Kitten, The Farm, The Real Thing, The Scaffold, Pete Wylie, The Christians, I:Candy, Eton Road, Micky Finn, Stan Boardman, Pete Price, Billy Butler, Ricky Tomlinson, Sue Johnston, Mike James Orchestra, Rubber Soul, X Tension dance group, Mick Miller, Mike and Jean at Party World, Joey and Marty Graney, Brian Oulton and Chesterfield High School, Lord of Liverpool Mayor Mike Storey, Neville Skelly, Roy Boulter, Marty Mullen, Francis Bentley, Steve Kelly, Kenny Dalglish, Craig Court, Mark Morgan, Paul and Joe Graney, Daniel O'Donnell, Kenny Graney, Blaine Tierney, our friends and neighbours and the people of Kensington, every single person who held a benefit night for the campaign, Kevin Georgeson, Peter Hooton, the young people of the city who showed their support throughout, everyone who joined Facebook groups supporting the campaign.

Greg O'Keeffe for putting my thoughts into words and all his support.

I'll never forget the generosity of the city of Liverpool and beyond. There are too many people who helped to mention them all. I could fill another book.

I'll always be grateful to you all.